CROSSING THE MAGINOT LINE AS A FORWARD ARTILLERY SPOTTER

ERICH WOLFRAM VON BLEICHERT

(1905-1991)

Copyright © 2007 by Erich Wolfram von Bleichert.

ISBN: Hardcover   978-1-4257-6779-2
                  Softcover   978-1-4257-6778-5

Translated from German by Rolf von Bleichert
Edited by Peter von Bleichert

Released by PvB Enterprises, Inc.
Redwood City, California, USA.

This book was printed in the United States of America.

To order additional copies of this book, contact:
Xlibris Corporation
1-888-795-4274
www.Xlibris.com
Orders@Xlibris.com
39718

CONTENTS

We learn to understand; we understand to prevent.

The forward observer with his wireless operator (author wearing cap).

CHAPTER 1

THE BEGINNING

Since May 10th, the day our armies invaded Belgium and Holland, we followed with fervor the progress of our comrades at the front's northern sector, proving their fighting spirit and abilities acquired in extensive preparatory training. Day and night, we listened enthusiastically to the radio about their successful campaign and their unbelievable accomplishments: How they have stormed through Holland, Luxembourg and Belgium, the tremendous effort at the Dyle Fortifications during the breakthrough at Liege! The energy with which they broke through the line at Sedan, after a short-lived but heavy resistance by the enemy, and pushed the English and French towards the channel coast in a magnificently conceived outflanking maneuver! Our spirits surged with every report, with any bit of news. However, it also increased our impatience wanting to finally participate, after the long, long months of waiting—to also be allowed to fight.

Secretly, everyone feared that nothing would be left for us to do, if the progress continues like this. After all, we also would like to join in.

One day, we too received our marching orders. For a short spell, we experienced real war for the first time. There were the annihilating bombardments by our own and the defending fire of the enemy's artillery; with attacks and blowing-up of bunkers, with counter-attacks and bombardments of newly occupied villages and forests; with larger numbers of prisoners and sorrowful losses from the ranks of our own comrades. Nearly four weeks passed since we had a taste of this fighting spirit and intoxication of conquest. Now, again, we are being held in reserve.

At the time, it was the week of Pentecost; we dislodged during a five-day attack the French from their trenches, in which they had faced us at Saarlautern during a long winter and an even longer spring. We pushed them back approximately 5 miles to the bunkers and fortifications of the Maginot Line. Being anxious to prove to our comrades in Belgium and northern France that we equaled their aggressiveness and fighting spirit, we were hoping that the time for a push through the Maginot Line had come. We could see through the stereo telescope from the B-Section (at the artillery the B-Section is the observation post from which the firing of the battery is directed) bunkers and other far stretching fortifications: threatening and still so inviting. Then we receive the order to withdraw! The front had been stabilized along the captured line. Our division is withdrawn for other purposes.

The battery is quartered in an idyllic village at the Saar. The orchards were in bloom, a brook murmured through a meadow full of flowers and the nightingales sobbed at night. Hardly anything reminds us of the war. Only the civilians are missing. We are in the restricted zone, which, for the last nine months, has been accessible to soldiers only. Occasionally, when for some special reason civilians were allowed to visit their homes in the village, the longing questions was always about the end, the day of their final return. And we promised them: Your exile from your homeland will end soon.

Our excitement increases from day-to-day, being informed daily—by radio and newspapers—about the achievements of the lucky divisions fighting the great battles in the north. When will it be our turn?

First, immediate readiness was demanded. Urgent preparation for the forward move should be made. Luggage is restricted to the most necessary items. All excess will be shipped back to the homeland via postal packages on trucks.

"You are needed in Belgium," we are told. However, the departure is delayed over and over, until there is hardly anything important left to do in Belgium. "We have been designated for sorties in northern Italy," was the next and somebody else knew for certain that the Balkans was waiting for us. Or is it Africa, perhaps?

The waiting becomes unbearable. Are we destined to sleep through the entire wonderful campaign in lazy comfort? Now, the exercises of the batteries start again, for the battalions of the whole regiment, with and without infantry, with and without the corps of engineers. The fighting against pillboxes and crossing of rivers is exercised, over and over again, in all possible variations. And in the meantime the others fight and are victorious in Flanders! We are shown movie collections of weekly newsreels covering the events in Holland and Belgium. Will it ever be our turn?

Now, finally, we too received our marching orders! During the night into the late morning we still had a great maneuver together with an entire infantry regiment: We routinely fire on and storm obstacles and bunkers of our own fortifications during our past weeks training. Still, in the evening at 11PM June 4th, the battery is ready to move out and with it the battalion, the regiment and the division.

We are to be employed in the surroundings of Saarbrueken. From there the thrust is to go due south right through the middle of the Maginot Line to Luneville, or so the rumor goes for days. For the time being we are moving southwards without lights in complete darkness. Strict discipline of each man is required. No cigarettes can be lighted and no flashlights can be used. The lights of the vehicles are off. Only the beginning and the end of the column are marked with weak white and red lights respectively. Under all circumstances, it had to be avoided to reveal the troop movements behind the front to the enemy's nightly reconnaissance flights. The drivers had to be very alert to minimize gaps between the vehicles in front of them. Otherwise, in the dark, the contact is immediately lost; following vehicles take a wrong turn; another column pushes into the breach created by the neglect.

All the platoons and batteries, supply vehicles and columns of the division—in total about 100 units—are gathering on the marching road from their divisional reserve station. An officer from division headquarters spots them into the mile long force just in the right sequence. That creates some delays. Over and over again the advance stops.

We hope the division will reach the new barracks before sunrise! Hour after hour passes. As we march through the streets of Voelklingen it gets light and the miners and foundry workers are on their way to work. Since their work is important to the war effort, they were allowed to stay within the restricted area and in the reach of the French long distance guns.

With the first rays of the morning sun, we are reaching our destination, a southern suburb of Voelklingen. It is high time that the troops disappear from the roads into their prepared barracks. The battery is positioning the guns and vehicles in a light maple tree forest, which prevents them from being spotted by enemy aircraft. The horses also stay in the woods. For this purpose long planks had been attached to trees by an advanced troop. The horses are tied to them in a long row. In addition, temperamental horses are separated by so called cross beams. For about four weeks and for the last time, the men are quartered in houses, sleep on mattresses in beds and dine on plentiful berries, which are ready to be harvested in the local gardens.

When will we get to the front? More waiting, one day follows the other. It is not possible to go outside of the houses and the woods. Over and over again French reconnaissance planes, searching for what is going on behind the German lines, appear suddenly over a hill or above the woods. They always will see more or less the same as for the last few months. Depopulated villages, smoking foundries, a few army horses working in the fields, some re-supply vehicles for the vanguard troops, maybe a few more trucks than usual on their way to the front.

Through out the night, trucks are carrying ammunitions; some times they even risk the trip during the day. All caliber ammunition is delivered in large quantities. Horse drawn ammunition vehicles move about as well, distributing the loads. While during the night cartridges and shells are stored in large piles behind the gun emplacements of the batteries targeted for firing, by dawn they are well camouflaged: hidden under trees, covered with branches, leaves and grass.

The most conscientious evaluation of the aerial photos taken by the French flyers could not find them.

The days of renewed waiting are useful in many respects; gun embankments and observation posts for the great attack are located and built. Officers travel to the front about 10 miles away. From high vantage points, they assess the terrain that must be bombarded and breached. We can see everything quite clearly from the church spire of Herschweiler, from the hill situated on the right side of the village, and from several sides of the woods facing the hills occupied by the French.

Our division is placed right in front of the first chain of the Maginot Line's fortifications. During the last weeks the infantry divisions on our flanks pushed from the frontier and have reached a point about six miles south of Saarbruecken. They encountered little resistance. However, attempting to break into the Line's bunkers itself without proper artillery bombardment should not be tried. We would clear the way for them but the fighting spirit of the French should not be underestimated. We took two outlying bunkers in the woods at the southward leading main road. Then the French heavy barrages hit the woods where they expected our attack to originate. Ricochets were everywhere as machine gun bullets from enemy bunker firing slots came uncomfortably near. They opened up on any movement at the edge of the woods. The attack is halted to avoid unnecessary casualties.

The first grouping of bunkers, which we see before us, protected by barbed wire entanglements and tank traps, was a tough obstacle. Such forts ran the length of the frontier! Distinguishable by the naked eye, however, the main fortifications behind it are stacked-up over several hills like theater scenes. Concrete pillboxes, tank cupolas and—in between—earth mounds indicating trenches and field bunkers. Such a sight!

Sketches of the enemy terrain are being made from various vantage points. They facilitate establishing the best suitable observation posts and the correct placement on our maps of the buildings recognized in the terrain.

The German push against the enemy is deepest just before Hill 304, which is covered with bunkers. Here the infantry took a fortification that lay in the open terrain about 600 feet from the edge of our woods. Only a few feet separated them from the first bunker on the hill. Here, following a standard blueprint for similar fortifications, the French connected two circular pillboxes of 6 to 9 feet diameter by a trench for a dumb-bell like outline. The earth walls are fortified by wire mesh. In the middle of each of the round stands is a post for the attachment of a light mortar. From the connecting trench an entrance leads to a roomy dugout, whose timber and earth cover could protect against shrapnel, but not against a direct artillery hit.

"That is where an artillery spotter should be sitting for the exact mapping and observation of the terrain we have in front of us" recognizes and orders the battalion commander. An officer is selected. He stays at the bunker of the infantry and at about midnight joins the platoon, going forward from the woods to relieve the advanced platoon in the captured field position. The French do not notice anything. Even so the machine guns aimlessly spray the foreground from time-to-time. However, they obviously did not think it possible that 30 men could be positioned for days just outside of their famous Maginot Line bunkers looking at the cards they hold. Otherwise, they would have covered our new post with heavy machine guns and artillery.

The disadvantage of the absence of any type of night reconnaissance becomes obvious; even during the night the French do not dare to come out of their fortifications.

"Our two advanced scouts, who during the night go up to 600 feet further towards the bunkers, have not once encountered a French reconnaissance patrol," stated the platoon leader. We made similar observation during the winter perimeter skirmishes. Whereas the German scouts penetrated nightly the enemy lines for hours at a time, the French hardly ever dared to pass their own front barbed wire entanglements.

Lieutenant Haeberlein stayed for 24 hours at the advanced observation post. Then he was relieved by his old battery comrade, Lieutenant Warning, for an equal period. They brought back maps of the target terrain with bunker locations, details on the movements between these locations and the enemy rear, all of which was very valuable information for the effective utilization of our heavy guns. The intelligence was equally important to division and army headquarters.

The waiting time at Voelklingen came to end. On the fourth afternoon: finally a meeting with the commanding officer. Then came the order: Under cover of darkness the division will move to its prepared firing positions. We are moving out at 2000 hours. Until night time a distance of 600 feet is to be kept between guns during the advance. Guns are to be ready for firing by 0400 and completely camouflaged against planes.

Drivers pack their bags, gunners: their back packs. Saddling, harnessing and hitching. The entire front along the Lorraine border, which here at the Warndt-District protrudes far in the north-south direction, will be on the move. At the left, beyond the border valleys, appear the first destroyed French villages, bombarded mostly by the French themselves. We are told that their artillery heavily bombarded all villages a few hours after they were lost. Later on, we were able to verify this for ourselves. From a heavily damaged spire suddenly ring bells. Soldiers stationed there must be ringing them. The gunners listen, thinking of the homeland they look at the brilliant evening sky. But the march continues . . .

In a meadow next to the road lies the fuselage of a downed French airplane. At the roadside of the last German village stands a captured tank recognizable from the large painted French cockade. Motorized troops are passing. Then we cross the old border. From here onwards all bridges have been blown up. In addition, craters large enough to accommodate a small house, gape in the middle of the road. The engineers have already erected emergency bridges and leveled ways to circumvent the craters. The detours are wide enough for just one vehicle and on-coming traffic delays our convoy.

By now it is night. The battery marches in closed ranks. While taking a break, we are passed by 21cm howitzers. Amazement runs through the convoy with anticipation of the things to come. The enormous guns are hauled in three sections, each on one separate carrier pulled by its own tractor unit.

The howitzers are to be stationed behind the next village. The village's main street is hopelessly blocked. The convoy cannot negotiate the narrow curve at the village entrance as one tractor unit skidded to the side. Our convoy stopped in the middle of the village, amongst the craters, which resulted from the nightly French bombardments. When will it start tonight? We had orders to clear the village as fast as possible, as experience has shown that bombardments were especially frequent at this location. Just here we had to be slowed down by a traffic jam and be forced to wait almost an hour. Finally, the blockage ahead of us is partially cleared. The howitzer clears the lane for us to pass. Half an hour later we hear echoing reports; it is the bombardment of the village we just had left.

The firing location has been reached. It is a slightly sloping meadow with rows of fruit trees bordered by woods about half a mile away. The cannons have to be unloaded, assembled and readied for firing. Due to their heavy weight, we transported them on the march in two parts: the barrel on a special carriage—drawn by six horses—followed by the frame carrier, also drawn by the same number of horses. Before leaving the road the barrels are heaved from the carrier onto the frame carriers. The assembled cannons are positioned at location. The barrel carriages then retreat about 3-3/4 miles back to a depot, a forest outside of the reach of the French bombardments.

There is hurried activity in the nightly embankment. Spades are flashing, axes are sounding in a distance above, trees waver in the dark, and scythes cut rustling through the grass.

At dawn, it was impossible to see the firing embankment of our heavy howitzers. A new row of large fruit trees was now growing in front of the other rows. It was impossible to distinguish guns under the forms covered with branches and grass or ammunition dumps under the grass heaps below the next row of trees. The meadow has been mowed in a wide circumference to eliminate any signs of our movements. Under a tree stands a sentry next to a small tent. Inside the tent his comrades-of-the-watch sleep until their turn comes. Otherwise nothing can be seen. If the enemy holds true to his patterns, the reconnaissance planes will soon come.

CHAPTER 2

READINESS

What happened to the men of the battery? We find them in the woods at a well deserved breakfast. They eat in front of the firing embankment at the time when the sun already reaches the ground of the forest through the light tree canopy. A camp has been set up not far from the battery and among the trees, in a less dense spot, somewhat of a clearing. About a dozen tents are grouped in the space. That is were the men are sitting on anything available in front of a table-like construction, salami sandwich in hand, steaming coffee in their mess tin. The field kitchen in a nearby and at work. The sun shines on the troopers naked torsos. The communication specialist, wearing the headsets of the wireless field radio, is reading aloud the copied messages. In the middle of the camp two barrels of beer, which the chief had arranged to be brought along, are waiting for consumption. In spite of the sleepless night the morale is excellent. After all, tomorrow or, at the latest, the day after that, the action finally will start again!

As observation officer, I am on my way to check out the observation post, which has been assigned to me at the edge of the opposite woods by the section adjunct. The edge of the woods can be observed from the opposite village and the bunkers on the hill on its right side. The distance to the next bunker is only about 1,800 feet. Sharp shooters and a machine gun are firing intermittently at believed targets or just to remind us that they are there. If there is movement at the edge of the trees the French artillery too will shoot a few salvos once in while.

At the assigned section near the edge of the woods the scouting observation officer crawls from bush to bush, trunk to trunk, way in front of the infantry's point. I finally find a suitable spot. At the edge of a path running parallel to the direction of the front stood a large maple. From behind the maple I overlooked the entire enemy terrain. The bushes in front provided enough protection against being spotted. The ditch of the path could be deepened as foxholes, which could protect the observation crew in case of bombardment. Once the observation post—O-Section—was established, the ditch would also provide a hidden approach. The trunk of the maple served as the corner post for a covered observation stand in which the observer with a stereo telescope could remain even under the heaviest bombardment.

The construction of the O-Section continues as dusk breaks. The stereo telescope—or rain pipes—is placed directly next to the tree trunk. A chest-high log wall is built in front of the position and covered with dirt. Brush and branches interfering with field of vision are removed. Several foxholes are started, small and deep with vertical walls. One is for the observation officer and one for the wireless operator who connects us to the firing embankments and the operational command. The dug out for the wireless operator is placed a bit further back from the observation post. We are able to utilize an old infantry trench for this.

Early in the morning of the next day, we appreciate the necessity and usefulness of the holes. Sitting at the stereo telescope, I am enjoying the breaking day. Once in a while a light battery is firing rapidly, barking salvos into the hinterlands. The shells take their singing path high above us. Then they start again. However, this time it comes in lower and frighteningly close to our position. There are the bursts, one right above us at the edge of the woods, nearly concurrently one behind us in the woods and one to the left. I leap with two jumps into the foxhole and squat on the very bottom! The barrage continues, exploding in fast sequence around us. Shrapnel is hitting through the branches and leaves close by, shot off branches and leaves are floating towards the ground. Good Lord, this one must have hit right next to the hole, I thought. The ground quivers and from the embankment a shower of dirt rippled back into the hole. As suddenly as it started it was over. Relieved but still anxious, I crawled out of the hole and cleaned off my shirt and trousers. What has happened to the stereo telescope? Right, there it is, but without its tripod. Behind it is a crater large enough for a man to crouch in. Some wood splinters are sticking from the ground. This is the remainder of the tripod on which the stereo telescope used to be mounted. However, disregarding a few paint scratches the actual telescope and especially the lenses were not damaged. Well, we were lucky! By wireless, which survived the barrage in its entirety, I order the observation aid to bring along a tripod when he comes to relieve us. Until then the field glasses—the double glasses—will have to suffice.

There was a lot to be observed on the opposite side at the French positions. The exact course of the barbwire and the tank obstacles had to be marked on the map, to enable us to shoot breaches into them before the attack by the infantry. The numerous dugouts and trenches, which represented together with the bunkers at the edge of the village a well camouflaged defense system, had to be found and their location entered on the map. The network of trenches, which connects the fortifications and lead back behind the line are being scrutinized over and over again to find a moving helmet, a lock of hair or even a naked torso glistening in the sun. Or whether further entrenchment is being prepared recognizable by the periodically appearing shovel and dirt at the edge of the trench. The French are acting very carelessly. They truly seem not to know what to expect. In the second bunker grouping lying further back, they walked back and forth in the bright sunshine, from bunker to bunker, across the meadows and fields, which did not offer any protection. At certain times soldiers gather from all sides coming at a bunker situated in the middle, most likely to receive orders from their commander. Once in a while one could see a truck on a far road or a small armored tread-vehicle, by which the French re-supplied the advanced fortification with ammunition and provisions.

All of these observations are reported back to headquarters. They allow estimates of the strength of the enemy, the distribution within their fortifications, time and frequency of guard changes and other details, which could be important for the strategy of attack.

At the camp in the woods a directive from the regiment headquarters is received: "The attack will be delayed until further notice!" This is a great disappointment. Is it possible that they did not make the anticipated progress at the northern section of the front? Or is France about to fall and we will not be needed at all? For the time being we have to wait again.

At the observation post our time is put to good use. We become more and more familiar with the enemy territory and with everything built there. Every night we work hard. The dug outs are made deeper and are covered with thick logs and dirt for protection against the 'tree exploders' much feared by woodland positions. These rounds explode by just touching the top of the trees and discharge blast of wood splinters from above. The dug outs are connected by trenches enabling us to go from one to the other without being seen. A protective trench in triangle shape is built around the newly erected stereo telescope, into which the observer has to crawl in from beneath, which might be a little bit uncomfortable. The walls and ceiling consist of double layers of logs affording a good protection against shrapnel. To keep the French from noticing the entrenchment during the quiet nights, trees could not be cut in front, corner posts could not sank in, nor was any sawing or hammering possible. Tree trunks are carried forward from far behind the lines and artfully stacked and tied with heavy wire. After five nights all of our preparations have been completed.

The gunners at the embankments are not idle either. Behind each mortar there were three dug-outs, some of which, however, were not even three feet deep due to the ground water level of the soggy meadow. Firing logs of all possible targets have been logarithmically computed and re-checked several times. Here too, everything is ready.

The waiting at the camp in the woods grew more and more difficult. There is an apparent deflation of moral. Even so the weather is bright and dry initially. The expectation of a major attack from day to day gives way to tension, resulting in irritability of the men. The continuing heavy and steadily increasing bombardment by the French artillery of depots and connecting roads to the back does not help.

In the sector of our division more than 25 enemy batteries are recognized. Especially the villages and street junctions receive regular attention, but also the woods are sprinkled over. Lighter guns are firing in unbelievable fast sequence salvos of 30, 40 and 50 shells. They must have automatic or semi-automatic loading devices.

Medium size guns, mostly two firing at the same time, are surprisingly accurate on selected targets. One evening, five out of 12 shells fired at the church spire of the next village, on top of which was an observer, were hits. This is a very good average for the artillery considering the great deviation factor. The fork in the road at the north entrance of the village is closely surrounded with deep craters, although, it most likely cannot be seen from the other side.

The heaviest shells roar in mostly from the far right, in all likelihood from mortars of the Maginot Line fortifications. Here and there they tear enormous craters, large enough to accommodate an entire gun crew.

With greater frequency we hear about losses caused by the French artillery bombardments. The night before, an anti-tank position in a wood was hit. They reported four dead and ten injured. Yesterday there were a few injured at the heavy battery embankment behind us. Today a command vehicle of the regimental communication service was destroyed. The entire crew and all horses except one perished. The next day it was again the turn of the communication group. During the night their encampment just left of our own received ten hits, which exploded in the crown of the trees and sprayed the tents in a hail of shrapnel. It is a miracle that there were only six or seven soldiers wounded. A heavy battery was badly damaged. It lost the larger part of its horses by a bombardment. A motorized unit, which came directly from Dunkirk and had participated in the great battle of northern France, had to mourn their first dead here.

Tempted by the warm sun and despite the risk of being spotted, the men removed their shirts and lay on the meadow near the edge of the woods.

In the afternoon a plane flew over the woods and two hours later their camp at the edge of the trees was attacked. A single 15 cm shell exploded in the tree canopy over thirty-two men who were having their supper while sitting on and around a tractor unit.

We ourselves were lucky. Small shrapnel hit only a young cadet officer in the left hand, while on guard duty at the guns. A laughable injury, but serious enough to take the poor chap back to the hospital and to cheat him out of the great adventure of the attack for which he had longed. Simultaneously shrapnel hit an ammunition dump. But only two boxes of cartridges caught fire and burnt with a bright flame. It burnt out after a few minutes. During the night and sometimes also during the day nearby exploding shells put the camp into a state of anxiety. Then we congregated in the shrapnel proof bunkers at the edge of the camp, which were built as defenses by the French. The bombardments resulted in one more inconvenience: The field kitchen detail—which brings the provisions and the eagerly awaited mail daily from the depot—would be late or not come at all!

During the fourth night I was fast asleep next to the battery commander in a tent. He was a lieutenant and commanded the light battery situated to the left of our unit. It had just had arrived yesterday. He was full of excitement. He had just returned from the front where the infantry had withdrawn. The French are attacking! He was absolutely certain that in front of us was no further protection and consequently we are now the front line. He had assigned his men equipped with rifles to deserted French trenches running across our camp. They were to await the attack there. The French are bombarding behind us preventing reserve troops from coming forward.

Fortunately our chief stayed calm in the face of these exciting developments. Even though the French artillery fire was heavier than before, we did not hear a single rifle shot with the exception of a machine gun far to the left in the sector of the neighboring division. In addition I had just returned an hour ago from the front, where we had finished the entrenchment of the observation post. I did not see anything unusual. I suggested to my chief that I would look one more time myself together with a non-commissioned officer and a bombardier to make sure whether or not the infantry was still in their foxholes.

When we stalked up to them, cocked rifle at hand, we found them all in the same places as every day before. They did not know anything about a French attack. An artillery guard at the very tip of the woods told me of the lieutenant's visit a short while ago during which they had heard several times suspicious rustle in the bushes in front of them. We listened for a while. There it was again. An obvious rustle, but a rustle which one could hear any night in the woods. A hasty mouse or some other small animal!

Half an hour later we continued our interrupted sleep with a lullaby of explosions courtesy the French artillery. Shells whistled and roared high above us as we asleep.

On the sixth day of our hold out in the woods, we had rain. It started early. Initially a sprinkle, which increased to an outright downpour, and continued all day with changing intensity. In spite of the draining ditches the water seeped from below into our tents by midday. Anybody who had to work outside was drenched to the skin and our proudly-built dugouts filled with water to the rim.

The O-Post in a wheat field. The observer communicates directly with the firing position by chest microphone and headset.

On the rain pipes; the stereo telescope minimizes reflections.

CHAPTER 3

THE ATTACK

On this terrible day, while we were wading through mud and water looking for something dry in our soaked bags, we receive the order to attack.

Shortly after 12 o'clock the battery chief received the order at our woodland camp: At X-time tomorrow morning the softening barrage by the artillery will start with the bombardment of the entrenchment system on the hill to the right in front of us and the village of Cappel. Small squares on the map were assigned to each battery, which they had to soften up sequentially in preparation to be stormed. This would be followed by targeting of enemy obstacles to create breaches, and craters in front of the enemy entrenchment to serve as protection for the attacking infantry. Half an hour before our X-time the elimination of the enemy artillery is to begin by our long distance guns. One and one half-hour after X the infantry will attack. The time for X will be advised later.

There is great activity at the battery brains—the camouflaged command bunker. As fast as possible but still with quiet accuracy the 'calculators' prepare trajectories, aided by firing tables, firing plans and logarithmic tables. Firing schedules and ammunition types are then formulated for the selected targets. They make sure the entire firing range is covered and the own infantry will not be put in harms way by the unavoidable deviation of the artillery. Earlier they have also calculated the details for further enemy targets, which will have to be fired upon as the attack progresses. The officers of the battery check one more time all results, which are than organized in timetables and firing plans. Maps are compiled and the firing plans for the observation groups and their advanced spotters arranged.

After dark we have to restore the flooded dug outs of the observer post and the battery embankment. Drainage has to be dug as much as possible, but in the most part the water had to be bailed out. Thanks to the Lord, it has stopped raining! The French nuisance bombardment rages on, as during the previous nights.

"X = 0800 hours," is the top secret order. We could therefore sleep for another few hours. However, no sleep for some of us, either due to feverish expectation of the coming events or the shivers of cold from the sopping wet uniforms.

On June 14, roll call is at 0400. The gun crews depart for the firing locations where they prepare the ammunition and store it near the guns for easy accessibility. They have to take cover in the foxholes one more time. The sharp whistle of the lieutenant warned them. He had kept a sharp eye on the French firing, while the gun crew was working. They hardly had taken cover before it exploded and hailed all around them. About thirty rounds landed. Then the strikes moved into the distance. Nothing much had happened. A few more scratches on the guns, some additional mammoth craters in between and a whole lot of duds recognizable by the black pipes sloping into the meadow like oversized rat holes. The French ammunition is not of high quality. Maybe it is too old? Or are the French war industry workers so unskilled? We have noted earlier and ever so often the surprising number of their duds.

After our own bombardment had started, there were strikes one more time in between the guns. Hardly anybody noticed them over the heavy thunder of our own salvos and the zeal of the battery crew. We were lucky again.

By now we were located in the observation post at the edge of the woods. The battery chief is looking through the stereo telescope inside the shrapnel proof hut, which looks like a triangle log cabin with a flat roof through which the observation tubes protrude. In my capacity as the observation officer I am squatting next to the hut behind the large trunk of a maple also surveying through double glasses. Next to me in the log covered, now muddy, hole, in which I also could seek cover in case of bombardment, a radioman is crouched on line with the command bunker. On the other side is a similar dug out with a non-commissioned officer as an observation assistant and the radioman connected to the firing site ninety feet further back in their hole the wireless operators have installed their equipment and are also keeping in contact with the firing site. Even further back, two additional wireless operators and their equipment are in readiness to accompany me, the advanced spotter, later on with the attacking infantry, now waiting in readiness in their holes everywhere.

At the observation post everything has been prepared in advance of X-time. But at the present time nothing can be seen. At dawn, thick white fog covered the meadows in front of us and the rising hill with the first bunkers to the right; a precursor of a nice day. However, right now we could not see anything of the fortifications and the opposite village. The scheduled firing calibration of the guns and verification of the direction could not take place. We had to fire blind in accordance with our firing plans without being able to make corrections through observation. Generally, our aim should be correct. Our personnel have made all computation and, now, before beginning the action, they check one more time for interfering winds and temperature influences adjusted in accordance with the latest weather forecast of the meteorologists.

Count down: five more minutes to go! Three more . . . one more. At exactly 0730 there is a powerful swelling roar above us in the air. At the same time the thundering sound of hundreds of discharges reaches our ears. The sound of hundreds of explosions returned after a few more seconds, confirming that the shells had reached their targets and created havoc at the artillery embankments at and behind the French lines.

And now, the rolling thunder, the roaring, howling, whistling and swishing does not stop. It is no longer possible to distinguish the individual discharges and hits. It is a boiling and billowing, a swelling up and decreasing sea of sound; a sound hurricane, which even further increased half an hour later, when our battery started to fire on the nearby targets such as field bunkers and obstacles. Alone in our sector of about 2 miles, 72 batteries of all gauges were firing at the highest possible firing speed. There were long barrel canons of 10 and 15 centimeters up to the very heavy 21 centimeter howitzers and even some "thirty fives" and "forty twos". The neighboring divisions were similar. Helping from the rear there was one gun for every three infantrymen leading the attack. The enemy also returned the fire. We felt like we were under a dome of shells flying high, back and forth.

Suddenly the roaring noise subsides. Still a few straying discharges, whistling above us, exploding on the other side. Then there is an eerie, tension-filled silence. Everybody on the other side, who had taken shelter in bunkers and protected fortification from the annihilating bombardment, quickly emerged and took positions in trenches and dugouts, at machine guns and mortars in anticipation of an attack. However, a few minutes later the roaring symphony started all over again, with renewed force destroying everything not protected by meter thick concrete or deep in-ground fortification.

It continues for forty minutes with undiminished force. And now the muffled roll and thunderous drone and howling whistling on both sides is mixed with the barking sound of the light long barrel guns, the anti-aircraft and tank canons, which had taken position at the edge of the woods under the protection of the artillery salvos. Now they are aiming from their open placements directly at the firing slots of the bunkers, slowly emerging from the fog.

To the right a tractor unit pulls an anti-tank gun through the woods. They position themselves close by—the black uniformed fellows. There: a nearby whistling, an explosion drowning the ongoing noise, flying dirt and bushes and smoke. Another shell, fired by the desperately defending enemy artillery, hits at our corner. In spite of the heavy bombardment of their own position, they also hit us.

Jumping into the foxhole, I am shouting and waving to the men of the anti-tank gun to take cover. The tractor unit is backing up during the bombardment. Until it stops, the blacks shirts are crouching safely with us.

Then they jump out intending to push their gun by hand to the very edge. But they cannot get it up the slope. Three of us are lending a hand and in no time it is in position. After a quick glance and adjustment of the targeting it fires. The tracer clearly shows the path of the shell towards the main firing slot of the "ear bunker" (named after its two protruding white side walls looking from the front like two enormous ears). The shell hits its target. Concrete pieces are flying around the firing slot. But now it has to be the slot itself. The steel slider seems to be closed. They will be unable to open it again after the shells have pounced on it!

With the field glasses it is possible to see clearly the results of the firing slot bombardments. Next to it the "new bunker," which is still surrounded by parts of scaffolding, water barrels and sacks of cement, is certainly out of action. The same fate for the third in the group, the "black bunker," which protrudes threatening out of the bushes with its black camouflaged walls. In many places the barbwire entanglements seem to be torn up by the heavy bombardment and the tank obstacles show breaches as well.

To the left appear flames through the steadily thinning fog. The village is burning. The hill of bunkers and the village are ready to be stormed. The salvos of our artillery are partially stopped and partially re-directed further ahead into the enemy territory. And there is the first infantry at the bottom of the meadow. Quickly they charge forward, hit the ground and continue to run. More and more appear. At the right as well they are approaching the bunker. Machine guns sound off. Individual hits are seen as white smoke between the attackers. Obstacles are blown-up.

Now, my time has come too. A shout to my communication crew, a handshake with my chief and we depart. First about 150 feet through the entanglement of fallen old maples, bushes and thorns, which are lying before the woods. The French had cut down a wide strip of forest to enlarge the firing range of their fortifications and for better surveillance of the woods behind it. Then we went down to the meadow, because the bombardment was heavier on the street leading to the right on the hill. Two radiomen followed me as fast as they could with their heavy backpack equipment. The radio crew is laying a cable a few hundred feet behind us.

As the forward observer, I must reach as quickly as possible the opposite slope of the hill in front of us with the infantry, to direct from there the fire of the battery to the targets lying behind the hill, which cannot be seen from the old observation post. We are crossing the meadow with large leaps. Infantry is ahead of us by six hundred feet. A few hits in the larger area around us, once in a while the whistling of machine gun bullets, otherwise not much resistance. There is the first wounded. A short question, an encouraging hello. Yes, he has been bandaged already. The medics will take him back soon. There is also a wounded Frenchman, who has dragged himself to this point. He too is wearing an emergency bandage already.

We soon reach the precipitous slop. Here the enemy seems to be firing more. I am waiting in a trench for the radioman to catch up with me. A hum in the air caught my attention. Correct, the Stuka (dive-bombers) have arrived to knock out the heavy bunkers of the main fortification. They are circling and apparently trying to locate their target through the mist, which still hangs over the ground. Suddenly one of the proud birds is in bright flames and going into a spin. Burning and dragging a black cloud of smoke behind him, he spins towards the ground. Faster and faster until he disappears behind the trees. What a shame! We did not see any smoke from exploding anti-aircraft fire in his surroundings. Did the French fire at him with machine guns? At the height in which he circled, it would have been an unbelievable shot in the dark. Or was it a mechanical failure, which caused the fire? I decide I will never know.

What is that above me? Is another airplane crashing? He is sliding sideways over the wing. He is initiating his destruction bringing nose-dive. Above his own infantry?! That is not possible. The bombs are falling! One can clearly count the explosives detaching themselves from the fuselage of the plane: One, two, three. I do not look any longer. I dive into the trench at which I was standing, mouth wide open with my forefingers in my ears. Then comes the explosions. I do not know, how many. The ground is shaking. There is a bursting roar, which does not want to stop. Or does it only echo in my ears? Clumps of earth and stones are coming down. For a short while it sounded like the gallop of horses. After a while I get up and look around. It seems the hits were over there at the road. Infantrymen are running to this area. Somebody screams. Now, they are carrying somebody away. Thank Heaven, the damage was not great. Our first taste of fratricide.

How could that happen? As I was told later by an infantryman, the bunkers, near which the bombs dropped, had just been taken through a courageous attack of a 1st Lieutenant with just a few men. The infantry had advanced much faster then anticipated by the flyer based on the time schedule of the plan of attack. It was hardly possible to recognize the few German men from above, especially since the mist restricted clear sight. And in the short time it had not been possible to put down demarcations of our position for our Stuka's to see.

What happened to my signalmen? Here are the radiomen, unharmed but out of breath. At the last moment they were able to guard themselves from the flying debris. One of the signalmen, however, is injured on his leg and is left behind in the care of the medics. The other one has to work on his own for the time being.

Now, I dash up the hill accompanied by the radiomen. At the top we go through some brush which has a trench in front of it. In we go. I can completely survey from here the two forest sections, which are the battalion's next goal of attack, which we have to support. The radiomen are ordered: "Set up here." As per the standard firing plan, the firing orders are prepared for the most important targets in the forest. In the meantime, the radiomen have established contact with the battery. My first question is whether the battery is ready for this advanced spotter. After a few minutes the battery is at my disposal.

As a starter, I have them one after the other concentrate fire on two corners of the forest from which stronger resistance could be expected. Shots on target are noted by the battery officer, which enables him to commence the real bombardment of the forest corners with everything at his disposal. Then I have the battery cover the two forest sections with twenty scattered shots each and advise the necessary corrections. All rounds hit the forest. They must inconvenience the French. In between I am giving a progress report of the attack to the battery chief by radio and confirm that the entire hill is free of the enemy. The main observation post has now to be moved forward.

The battery now received firing orders directly from the unit commander, so I utilize the break to scout a suitable location for the new forward observation post. I find it in a well finished trench, which may have housed a mortar at one time. From here one could see at the left the captured village of Cappel and the entire terrain, which is now being defended vehemently by the French. The trench will be sufficient protection for the entire observation unit. I am sending back a radioman to a rendezvous point agreed upon with the chief, to guide the forward coming men.

In the meantime, it is midday . . .

Using empty ammunition crates as furniture, I am getting comfortable at the new post with a piece of bread and some salami. By using the field glasses, I try to assess the current status of the battle. The village to the left, burning at many places, is completely in our hands. However, at the nearby southerly running main road from Strasbourg to Metz little progress is being made. Our men have all reached the road, which is running on a low ridge. If they try to cross the road, they are exposed to the fire from the fortification on the other side, which apparently suffered very little damage. Amongst them the black block of bunker 987 looks especially threatening.

The enemy artillery is also firing heavily again, especially at the village exits and around the church. While the Stuka's are wonderful to watch, displaying searching circles and rapidly following dives, their hits and enormous dust columns are far away on the fortification line in the enemy rear. Either they believe that the frontline has advanced much further forward or they do not dare to target the nearby bunkers in consideration of their own infantry that move close by. For the same reason our artillery is unable to bombard the main pockets of resistance. For the time being the attack has come to a halt here.

Some lightly wounded infantrymen are searching the many bunkers around us for lost Frenchmen. The suffocating dark caves are built deep into the slope steeply falling from the village, and on which our new observation post is located. For eight long months, they provided to the French garrison a safe if not healthy and comfortable shelter, in which they played cards, drank red wine and ate chocolate on white bread. At least this is to be concluded from the items and provisions found there.

The prisoners, who are now taken out of the caves two or three at a time, confirm this conclusion: For the entire time they served they had no regular duties—such as training, schooling, or working. Maybe once in a while weather permitting they did some entrenchment work. They were told to stay put in their caves and bunkers for one, two, or even three years. By then the war would have been won by itself. No wonder, they have no fighting morale.

And what do they look like, how are they equipped? Just now a larger group is returning from the village, again guarded only by one lightly wounded soldier. On stretchers they are carrying three or four heavy wounded comrades. They stop here for a brief moment. The heavy bombardment still shows on their faces. Or is it fear of imprisonment, of which they were told the worst stories? We can reassure them in reply to their worried questions. In spite of the hot temperature they wore coats or in their absence woolen cardigans. Then we found out that the entire troop had not even been issued jackets! Other units had jackets but no coats throughout the entire winter. Boots and pants are similarly uncoordinated. In comparison to ours their helmets look like tin toys. Is that the 'best army of the world,' for which the French taxpayers had to raise enormous annual sums over the last twenty years? What has happened to all the monies?

Conversing with them they open up a little bit more, realizing that we are friendly and plan to neither mistreat nor rob them. Quite a few men from Alsace-Lorraine are among them. They hope to see their homeland very soon again. Even the true Frenchmen did not hide their joy that the war was over for them. "La guerre c'est finie," they say smiling.

The captain and the rest of the observation unit arrive at about 1400 hours. The stereo-telescope is mounted. All preparations for the firing control are made quickly. Also, the wire connection to the battery finally works and is far more reliable than the wireless. In the afternoon we are firing either independently at recognizable enemy targets (like firing mortars and entrenchment), or with the rest of the unit at the still resisting line of bunkers beyond a big road.

The infantry is still stuck. At times they even had to retreat from the heaviest fortification, bunker 987, to allow the bombardment of this bastion by the heavier artillery. One direct hit destroyed the back part. However, in the front are still two machine guns controlling a wide swath of the main road.

Now our battalion is again grouping between village and road under the protection of the ridge running parallel to the highway. We see the men lying closely to each other on the sloping meadow, partially in quickly dug holes, partially in craters, which resulted from the intermittent French bombardments. From the left we see three columns of a reserve company. They split up into squads and then merge with the assault troops.

As the forward observer, it is high time for me to report to the forward battalion operation post with which we are working together. I give the radio and signalmen the direction: To the left of the church along the cemetery across the meadow to the white house on top of the ridge close to the road. From there I have to look for the operation post.

I sprint up the slope to the edge of the village in large leaps. In the midst of a crater field created in the morning by our heavy guns, I am waiting for the firing at the square around the church to pause. Then I quickly cross the village; I am at the wall of the church square when the salvos started again behind me. I hope the signalmen will make it as well. I continue up the meadow slope. I jump from crater to crater. From somewhere at the side a machine gun is firing. Over and over I can hear the unpleasant whistling of the bullets.

I estimate another 240 feet to the white house from the crater in which I am catching my breath. Looking back, I can see the signalmen reaching the church wall and running into the meadow. Then, suddenly, it started at my end. In intervals of a few seconds the shells explode around me, sometimes near, sometimes further away, but all no further than three hundred feet from me. I am pressing myself as deeply as possible into a small crater, which just covers me and I feel fairly safe. Without interruption the firing continues. The minutes feel like an eternity.

The target seems to be mainly the side road, which connects to the highway at the white house. In between still is the vile singing of the machine gun. Ever so often I peek over the edge of the crater looking for the signalmen and the further away explosions, until a nearby hit causes me to lower my head again.

Finally this barrage of hell fire ended. I don't know how long it raged; was it half an hour, a whole hour, or even longer? I do not see my signalmen. I reach the white house with three long leaps. A medical dressing station has been established under its protection. It is not a pretty sight. The worst is the moaning of the wounded. I found out that the operation post was situated six hundred feet to the left in a finished French embankment. In case the radiomen made it, the sergeant of the medics was to direct them to it. During the conversation a few shells again are hitting behind the house and near the side road. Everybody presses himself against the wall of the house. Then I sprint from crater to crater across the meadow, along the highway to the gun embankments, there in front to the left. The neighboring division to the left occupies the first bunker. The second has been taken over by the operating staff of a light battery. In the third I could finally report to the battalion commander I was looking for.

The radiomen are not arriving. Without a connection to the battery, I am useless. I therefore started looking for them. The barrage has slowed down. Only the machine gun bullets are still whistling over the meadow. At the cemetery wall I find the cable rolls left by the signalmen. But there is no trace of my men. I go further back passing the church to the observation post.

I find them all there in good health. They had retreated when the barrages did not stop and the church square received again a few hits. The chief held them back to save them from the continuing bombardment of the village and the meadow.

Hot meals—noodles and beef—just arrived from the rear. Quickly I am emptying a mess tin. Then we march off, the radiomen and me. During the night the signalmen are to lay the cables. This time I am not leaving the radiomen on their own. We make it safely to the battalion operation post. By nightfall I could report that the wireless connection to the battery has been established.

Shortly prior to this, however, we have an exiting interlude. Some agitated machine gun operator thought he saw a white puff at the church bell tower of the taken village. Most likely shrapnel or a machine gun bullet hit against it, but he believed a sharpshooter was sitting up there and that the bullets whistling around must originate from there. Consequently, he is firing his machine gun into the window of the tower, but on the other side his bullets exit near an anti-tank canon, which is sitting there on the opposite slope. The anti-tank crew, thinking they were being sprayed from the tower. Their canon is trained quickly, and, in no time, tracers stream into the tower and out on the other side, quite visible in the dusk. Now, everybody is convinced that the enemy occupied the tower! A heavy bombardment starts against the innocent building. When the battalion commander called, "cease fire," there is nothing left of it.

The battalion operational post was crowded with officers and with dispatchers going back and forth. The relief of the battalion by another new battalion, which today was left behind in the woods as a reserve regiment, is being prepared.

The company leaders are reporting: The situation is not very good. Only parts of all three companies could cross the highway and not very far. None of the bunkers lying on the other side of the road could be taken. The continuous attempts have lightened up the companies. Many wounded are still lying in the barbwire obstacles and could not be rescued so far. A platoon leader, who courageously broke through, is pinned down with his men on top of bunker 987. All are more or less heavily wounded and are unable to withdraw as long as there is still daylight.

A captain with a shot-up right leg is sitting on a crate. His sullen face reflects the effort to overcome the terrible pain. Next to the neighboring gun embankment, in which a doctor feverishly is bandaging and giving first aid, are a number of bodies covered by tarpaulins. Nothing could be done for them any more.

And still, machine gun bullets are whistling about our ears the minute we step outside of the protective entrenchment. So far we were unable to locate from the firing gun on our flank. Most likely it is firing from a bunker to the left of the first trees of the neighboring sector.

In spite of the difficulties and the losses, the company leaders are full of piss and vinegar. They are convinced that during the night they would be able to take the bunkers they had failed to seize. The necessary engineering weapons are already on hand and during the night the bunkers are not able to protect each other.

However, as per orders of the regiment commander, the weakened storm battalions are to be replaced by fresh companies. This is also in view of the exertion to be expected tomorrow since today's considerably ambitious targets were not reached. We must progress tomorrow that much faster. The new company leaders have arrived. They are leaving now with the comrades they are replacing, to be briefed at location.

I have a situation report transmitted to the battery commander that is also for transfer to divisional headquarters. Then I find an unoccupied spot on the wet ground of the entrenchment. I crouched and slept well for a few hours in spite of the uncomfortable position.

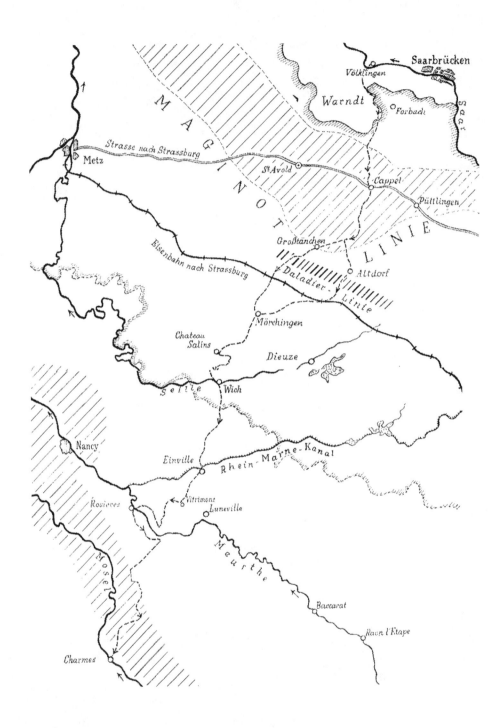

Map of the advance from Voelklingen to Charmes.

CHAPTER 4

BREACHING THE MAGINOT

On June 15 at 0200 I am waking up on my hard cold seat, disturbed by the commotion at the post caused by newly arriving news. The battalion commander informed me that Bunker 987, one part of which had been destroyed yesterday by the artillery, was now taken.

Enemy resistance apparently weakened in our and other sectors. The continuation of the attack has been scheduled for 0500 with the goal to completely break through the chain of bunkers and subsequently strongly pursue the enemy. The neighboring division to the left will start the attack as early as 0300. Under no circumstances were we to fire into the adjacent sector after 0300 in order not to endanger the storm infantry, which was expected to advance quickly.

Artillery preparations before the attack were not to be made to avoid alerting the enemy. It was hoped that surprise would lead to a faster result. However, the artillery was on stand-by in case it was needed during the attack to help in storming individual bunkers and entrenchment of unexpected heavy resistance.

I am waking up the wireless operator, but he cannot get a connection. Either the men are asleep on the other side or atmospheric disturbances are to blame as we are seeing summer lightening in the distance. Most likely both might be the case. After an hour of unsuccessful attempts and the equally unsuccessful waiting for a cable line, which had been promised me the previous evening, I realize that I was unable to accomplish my task this way.

For the fourth time I am taking the same path through the meadow and the village to the observation post. On the way back later on, it will have been the fifth time. At least the artillery is no longer firing and only the machine gun bullets are whistling around.

I found everybody fast asleep at the observation post, with the exception of two lonely radiomen each attending his equipment. After a little searching I am waking up the captain and the major. They and the remaining crew had found a comfortable place at a French medical post and slept soundly. I give my report and immediately request two signalmen to still lay a line to my post before the start of the attack. Following my report the major prepares himself to follow me to the infantry operation bunker. In the meantime I left with the two signalmen hurriedly. Exactly at 0500 we returned to the other side and a few minutes later the new connection was established.

Protected in some bushes, I watch the attack. It moves surprisingly fast. What is the matter with the French?

I report back by radio: "Our own infantry has reached the first woods south of the village Cappel. Bunker 915 has been taken. Company 2 is approaching the hill from the left of the woods, the 3rd from the right. Neither company encounters significant resistance. I myself with the signalmen try to connect with the left company. I have the signal troop lay the wires towards the southeast corner of the U-woods as a terminal. End."

The radiomen are ready. Forward! We would first move to the right towards the white house at the crossing. Then down under the protection of the gardens.

As soon as we step out of the bushes, a heavy machine gun starts shooting, the bullets are whistling through the air close by. We run down the meadow in leaps from cover to cover. The engineers have blown a hole through the strong barbed wire obstacle at the bottom. This sole passageway can be dangerous if the machine gun is trained on it. The reserve of the second company approaching from the right has the same opinion. They are setting off smoke grenades into the wind. The smoke drifts and envelopes the surroundings of this dangerous location. We too are quite able to pass through without difficulties.

The infantry is rushing the incline over there. I join them without consideration to the weighted down wireless operators ability to follow. I had to know in which direction the infantry was moving on the other side of the hill.

On top of the mount I stay back for a while to let the wireless operators catch up. The infantry is continuing to rush forward towards a burning village. The Great Forest is located behind it. Just now the first troops of the fiercely advancing company are approaching it without being shot at. It is 0715.

I look around. Everywhere are deep craters, collapsed trenches, and torn up concrete walls. We bombarded the area yesterday afternoon. I can even find the location from where continuous enemy mortar fire originated. The entrenchment, dug deeply into the ground, shored up by wickerwork and boards with a middle post for the mortar, is clearly recognizable. One hit pushed in a wall. However, at their retreat during the night, the French did not leave behind any equipment, wounded or dead.

The concrete heap there to the left apparently is an undamaged bunker, whose machine gun slot goes out to the other side. I am not sure why and I had to investigate more closely. I approach it avoiding the gun opening. A six-foot deep trench covered with wire mesh as camouflage leads to the back. About sixty feet from the bunker the wire mesh is torn. That is were I lowered myself into the trench and slowly moved forward. There is a heavy door ahead; it seems to be ajar. I better draw my pistol, I think and do. It is easy to push the door open. A short passageway appears. At the end it turns to the right. Dim light is coming from this direction. There was a scraping noise. I cock my pistol. "Is somebody there?" I shouted. At the moment I was not able to think of the French expression. There was no answer. Carefully I take three steps to the corner and look to the right. Quickly I pull back. In the incoming light from the gun opening were three figures in plain sight with one or more machine guns in front of them. I had my pistol in the left hand and fired! Ping, ping—two quick shots go into the concrete wall behind the figures followed by their wild cries of fear. I seem to understand something like, "Prisonnieres."

"Vous etes prisonniers! Haut les mains! Baissez les armes," I shout at them."

"Oui, oui, monsieur," I hear them reply.

"Suivez moi!" I still shout, and then I exited as fast as my dignity would permit back through the trench and climbed out of it with monkey-like speed. I had no intention to get close to the three guys and the machine gun down there in the narrow trench.

What happened to the wireless operators? Aha, there they are! I shout to them: "Drop the equipment and come here, double time!"

All three Frenchmen appeared in the mesh hole and surrendered. One after the other I allowed them to climb out and then had my men search them for weapons. All three of them looked pale and frightened. With tears in his eyes one of them showed me a bleeding scratch on his finger. He says reproachful: "Vous m'avez blasse!" He may have caught a little shrapnel from the pistol bullet ricocheting from the wall. How easily could I have hurt one of them more seriously, I realize with dismay.

With pride, one of the wireless operators takes the prisoners to the rear. They are the first to be captured by the artillery regiment. The other operator sets up his equipment and transfers my message about the rapid advancement of the infantry. I urgently recommend to the battery commander to immediately move the observation post and the firing embankment forward. The infantry will soon be at the outer rim of the reach of our guns. Accordingly, I order the signalmen, who just came out of the woods with their wire reels, to again pick up the line.

Until the return of the second wireless man transporting the prisoners, we have breakfast: In the backpacks abandoned at the bunkers and dug-outs, we find large quantities of chocolate and cookies. It represented apparently the ration of the troops. We welcomed it. These days we have not much time and opportunity to eat.

Finally the wireless operator returns. On the road of advance, on which the 3rd infantry regiment of the division, thus far held in reserve, is now moving forward in marching columns. We join them.

We no longer have to worry about enemy aircraft. Our air superiority is obvious. Not even reconnaissance planes are seen any longer. Motorized units—anti-tank cannons and light artillery—are passing the regiment and advancing to the front, always swinging towards the south. No more shots are fired. Even from the front nothing can be heard. The division seems to be pushing into a vacuum created by the skillful and quick retreat of the enemy. The breach through the main fortification is complete.

In the morning fog, a gun carriage is pulled by a team of heavy horses.

The 15cm schwere Feldhaubitze 18 (15 cm s FH18 (Immergrun)) is shown. This medium artillery piece formed the backbone of the German artillery force. The cannon were broken down into gun and barrel, each component carried by a six-team heavy horse carriage for maneuver. Once deployed, the warhorses and carriage retreated about four miles from the cannons, seeking cover of forests. One thousand seven hundred eighty-five horses served in each German artillery regiment. (Hogg, Ian V., "German Artillery of World War Two." Greenhill Books, London. 1997. Pg. 64).

A barrel carriage (Rohrwagen) travels through a conquered town following its respective gun carriage.

"Battery: fire!" commands the battery officer. The salvo roars. In front and to the left, expended artillery shell casings, to the right: ammunition baskets filled with waiting rounds.

The wireless crew is operational and issuing firing orders long before telephone crews have installed their cables.

The telephone operator connects the firing position, the firing command post and unit HQ.

The gunner: the battery's flexibility depends mostly on his unshakable calmness and dependable targeting.

CHAPTER 5

BREACHING THE SECOND LINE OF DEFENSE

To catch the spearhead of the infantry, my operators and I catch a lift first on horse drawn vehicles then trucks and tractor units of the forward pushing troops. We pass through the still burning village at the center of the fortresses of the main line, La Valette. The bombs of the dive bombers have done their work. An enormous crater gapes where a house and an entire farm had been standing the day before yesterday. At some spots the road is hardly passable.

The road is leading further south. The next village, Leyweiler, is completely intact. The evacuation of the civilians would not be necessary. At a crossing, the division's general surveys the hurried advance and the sequence of passing units in case of renewed resistance and the need for immediate engagement. The village of Altrippe is to the right. Then we pass through Hellimer, yesterday's original destination.

The marching route branches off to the left at Kreuzhof-Ferme. At this point the anti-tank cannons, which had taken us along for the last stretch, take position in order to protect the advance against possible tank attacks on the flank. On both sides of the road we can see the spread out infantry advancing; the vanguard battalion. There is a group of riders in front and to the left at the edge of the woods. They survey defensive positions for their battery. We just had passed the battery itself. It is positioned quite forward to support the vanguard in case of an unexpected enemy contact.

Now still a forced march by foot. The hot midday sun is scorching the road. As I am passing by I report to the colonel of the infantry regiment, who was comparing dispatches with the map at the edge of the road. The enemy seems to take position. A few shots are heard. The bicycle company reports a new bunker line behind the next village. This must be the so-called "Daladier Line," which the French supposedly have expanded last year.

For the time being there was to be no stopping. Dripping with sweat I finally reach the spear head and the commander of the vanguard battalion. We are about eleven miles from our morning starting point and about 23 miles from

Saarbruecken. It appears that the civilians were expelled from their farms only today or yesterday. The enemy troops also seem to have just left. Black spotted cows and wounded military horses are mixed up in the same corals. The fields are tended and promising an ample harvest. Here a dog is pulling on its chain; there a cat is sneaking along the house. The animals are noisy in their stalls. Although the cows have been given plenty of hay, their full udders needed to be relieved.

There: the first civilian since crossing the border. He is standing in the doorway of a cow shed with the milking pail in his hand, a tall Lorraine man with white hair. His greetings come from a laughing face. I savor the offered fresh milk. It tastes good! The first drop after many months.

"Where are all the others?" I asked.

"They all had to leave within the last two hours! Only I and old Rene and Henri were allowed to stay for the animals."

"Aren't you afraid of us?"

"Why should we be afraid of you? Yes, they have told us many things, a lot of horrors about the Germans. But I laughed at them. Why should we leave? I know the German soldiers!" With a cunning smile he pulls out of his pocked a black and red ribbon. His eyes gleamed with pride when he lifted on it the iron cross.

"Verdun 16th of July," he said with a pensive expression on his face. "Now I can wear it again."

I shook his hand, a look into the sparkling blue eyes. I have stayed too long already.

I am catching up again with the head at the southwest exit of the village. At his point it seems to get serious again. An extensive crater disrupts the road. The adjacent walls of two farmhouses have collapsed into it. The rooms and kitchen are in full view of the bystanders. The leading infantry just climbed out of this artificial valley. Appearing on the opposite rim, they reach with a few jumps the road, which continues between the fields. Then it begins, machine gun rattle, apparently from quite far away. But immediately the bullets clatter against the opposite house walls.

Seconds later a screaming shell rushed through the air and exploded in the gardens at the edge of the village with great noise and hurling earth high into the air. A welcome care of the French Artillery . . . In quick succession followed salvo after salvo. Everybody hurriedly takes cover. They push behind the house walls warding off the enemy, into cow barns with strong arched ceilings and into the few cellars. Thank the Lord, the bombardment falls a little short. Only one direct hit of a barn had resulted in wounded.

I am leaning against a house. My soldiers have made it as well. However, to them the latest discovery seems to be more important than the bombardment. Excitedly they are telling me that there are four French military horses around the corner in a barn, one of which is a magnificent heavy grey one. They wanted to have him haul a small wagon to carry us and our heavy equipment. Although he arrived later, a first lieutenant also laid claim to the four horses for pulling his anti-tank cannon.

I knew how heavy the wireless equipment would get on extended marches. In addition I wanted to do a favor for the foraging sergeant by acquiring a good working horse for the battery. Therefore, as soon as the bombardment died down a little, we hurried over there and lead the proud battle horse out of the barn. With its broad chest, strong neck and short cut mane that is what it really looked like. Thrown around in the dirt of the road are all sorts of harness from which I picked the most needed parts. Bridled, saddled and harnessed we were soon able to lead our 'Gaston' into a barn that was safer during bombardment. I pacify the first lieutenant, who appeared in the meantime, by pointing out the remaining three captured horses.

Unfortunately my companions, though trained as the best signalmen and operators, did not have much horse sense and the harnessing remained nearly exclusively my responsibility. Also the choice of a wagon, the selection of the harness ropes, but especially also the hitching and the breaking in of the animal. Gaston is not very appreciative of being harnessed into a pair of shafts and directed from the coach box by long leads.

While I broke the animal, the wireless operators erected their equipment and tried to establish a connection. The old observation post would be out of range by now. However, by now the relocation of the post may have been accomplished. Over and over they speak into the microphone: "Gustave—Emil—Paul! Answer! Please, come in."

Gustav—Emil—Paul, which was our battery code, did not reply. For the time being we had to wait, but would attempt contact every fifteen minutes. I needed to transmit my situation report.

I find the operation post of the vanguard battalion in a grassy garden at the village outskirts. Here one could move only on his stomach in order not to be spotted from the enemy occupied ridges. The harassing fire of the French, at this time, went mainly beyond the village allowing for an undisturbed development of a plan of attack here at the front.

Reconnaissance parties have established that we faced again a well-entrenched line of bunkers with gun turrets and embrasures. Apparently the embankments and dugouts in between were not completed. The commander is considering whether he should call in dive bombers and artillery for a thorough softening up of the area to reduce losses on our side.

However, the requirement of a quick continuation of the attack and advance was the decisive factor: we must utilize the existing means to breach the fortification and could not wait for Luftwaffe sorties.

The artillery could handle the job. A few batteries of light howitzers and also heavy long barrel guns were in position to start the crushing fire on the bunkers and anything else between and beyond, which would prove to be a worthwhile target. At dusk a surprise infantry attack was to take the main bunkers and to force the enemy to give up the line. This is exactly what happened that night.

CHAPTER 6

PASSING THE MARCHING COLUMNS BY MOTOR BIKE

For the time being I am returning to the village to meet up with my radio operators. My lieutenant colonel—the commanding officer of my artillery regiment—is just moving into his operation's headquarters. I give him a situation report about the vanguard battalion and the plan of attack and accompany him to the commanding officer of the infantry. Following my request he provides me with a motor cycle to drive back in search of my battery and division, since the operators still cannot raise them by radio. Carrying the order for the division to advance today as far as Kreuzhof-Ferme—about 1.9 miles from our present position, In the cycles side car, I take off with the driver out of the village.

We do not get very far. Shortly beyond the village outskirts, where the French batteries still cover the terrain, we had a flat. The spare tire is mounted by our combined efforts. Attack engineers shelter in the ditches next to the road. They are anxious to end their vulnerability and take their explosives and flame throwers towards the enemy bunkers. Frontline anti-tank cannons have taken position at both sides of the road are effective at responding to the French fire. They fire and tracers stream away. A French shell bursts close by.

Now we are ready to take off in our motor cycle again. Soon we are speeding along the endless columns of the marching divisions. There are units of three divisions on the same road of advance! Yesterday's heavy rains rendered all other roads impassable. For more than nine miles vehicles are bumper-to-bumper—light and heavy guns, ammunition carriers, armored vehicles of the infantry, heavy machines guns, field kitchens, large pontoons of the bridge construction engineers, communication vehicles, and motorized engineering units. Among them are the marching infantry and cavalry. Towards the end are the extensive supply lines made up of peasant-looking wagons under large tarpaulins. This caravan earned us at the name "Gypsy Division" at the frontline.

For nearly an hour we travel against this slowly moving column. I searched until finally seeing the head of our heavy division. There is the major! He welcomes me happily as the "runaway" missing since morning. I deliver the order of the regimental officer in charge and brief him on the situation up front. The division may have to march all night in order to reach the ordered temporary destination. Actual engagement at this location, however, may be unlikely. Until then, hopefully, the resistance of the rear defenses will be broken.

With great jubilation, I am unloading at my battery a carboy of delicious red burgundy. It would be refreshment at the next stop for the tired bodies, hearts and spirits. My operators had taken it for their comrades as booty at Altdorf. We go back another few miles to the village of Cappel to fill our tank at the newly established field gasoline station.

As soon as we return with our full tank to the main road of advance and are starting to pass the marching troops to reach my operators, something happens. It may have had a touch of humor, but became very embarrassing for some, in spite of its good outcome.

Shouting coming from the front traveled quickly along the road. Now it is possible to distinguish the call passed on by hundreds of voices: Tanks from the front! Shrieking sounds and hits as if the tanks were amongst us spewing death and ruin! We too are stopping and jump on the side of a crater a few feet away, in which we could take cover if necessary. Then I look around. What did actually happen? From the front a few horses are stampeding along the road, in between cavalry and soldiers on foot. They apparently have completely lost their minds and shout over and over, "Tanks, tanks!" I force some to stop and to explain their warnings. It is in vain. In the meantime the soldiers of the supply troop next to us also have dispersed in the terrain and camouflaged themselves as much as possible. The deserted horses are standing quietly and are enjoying the unexpected stop. Now somebody shouts, "Unharness the horses! Everything off the road!"

This is all nonsense! "The horses stay harnessed! The alarm is over! Everybody back to the vehicles!" I shout as loud as I can. We jump on the motor cycle and ride reassuringly past the vehicles. That it was a false alarm was accepted as quickly as the previous thoughtless tank warning.

But has it been a false alarm? It must have been! I have seen it myself that at the front the anti-tank cannons were in position. It would not have been easy to breach them. I have also seen how jammed the road has been; it was nearly impossible for the cycle to pass through let alone a tank. And it was impossible to attack through the dense and barbed-wire forest on both sides of the road. Most of all, how come we did not hear any shooting? Our anti tank cannons would be firing rapidly. And tanks usually do not pass enemy columns without utilizing their machine guns and rapid firing cannons. But not a single shot was fired. There were no flares, no red ones, a warning signal for tanks. It would have been impossible to miss them in the dark dusk.

At the very front there might have been tank warnings. Here at the rear, however, was no cause for concern, even less for a panic.

We learned later that even at the front there were no tank sightings. In spite of a thorough investigation it could later no longer be determined where the alarm originated. Maybe the order by word of mouth: "Anti-tank battalion to the front," which was meant to advance the anti-tank cannons for the bombardment of the bunkers, was mutilated by an over anxious dispatcher to "Tanks in front." The result was that the many miles long column panicked and nearly dissolved! The level headed action of some officers and some calm men's clear thinking trying to established order in the rear—same as I was doing—may have affected the nearby vehicles and groups, but did not prevent the alarm call from spreading like wildfire to the back nearly panicking the long stretched out column. Horses tripped, poles broke, and whole teams run away and disappeared in the darkness. Some vehicles tried to turn. The artillery took a defending position. Everything happened very fast. The officers traveling by car and motor cycle along the columns energetically pacified the troops and prevented a general panic. But, even so . . .

During my many efforts to pacify, to re-establish order, to continue the march, I encounter an officer, a major, who is trying the same. We exchange a few words, are taken aback—a happy recognition. In spite of the masking helmet, I recognize the good friend of my father. A few months ago I heard of his transfer to my division. But in spite of all attempts I had been unable to locate him so far. He is the commanding officer of the division's supply line and is happy that he got his unit through the alarm more or less intact. Since there is no chance tonight that I could still reach the front via the jammed road, we sit down next to the street at the edge of the woods for a "cold supper," which is spiced by the exchange of old memories and the latest adventures.

At dawn we get on the bike, my driver and I, after a deep and refreshing short sleep on the floor of the forest. The columns are again orderly. The one side of the road is clear for the drive to the front.

We have the same bad luck as yesterday. A few hundred feet after the start we have to stop with a flat tire. This time we have to dismantle the tire and repair it as the spare we used yesterday.

During the repair work—I am hardly able to assist the driver—I am inspecting a large nearly undamaged bunker, which was close to the road and commands a wide clearing running diagonally through the forest. Inside were nearly thirty mattresses stacked in twos, indicating the housing of a large garrison. The armament included one rapid firing cannon and three heavy machine guns, swivel-mounted on a firm base. An inside well operated by a hand pump secured the water supply. I cannot find any anti-gas air filtering system as we have seen them on the Western Line. In view of the large span the concrete ceiling appears very weak. It could hardly stand up against a direct hit by one of our guns.

At an ante chamber I find an empty officer's trunk made from tin for use in the tropics. I could make good use of it to replace my chest, which was on the brink of falling apart. Also the hardly worn rubber boots will come in handy. I put the calling card of the former owner, a French lieutenant, into my pocket. Maybe in the future, I will be able to return or replace the items.

Horses are now led out of the forest. They are French military horses with their typical flat noses, straight falling croup and brush-like manes.

From the road soldiers run down into the forest while others return with canteens, blankets and other outfit equipment. What is going on down there in the woods?

Darn, this looks bad! Right on the edge of the woods is a long row of smoked blackened frames of burnt-out trucks. Except for a few pitiful remains all coachwork and tires were totally burnt. The steel components are wildly bent and twisted by the heat, the chassis, axles and motors smashed by explosives and pierced by shrapnel.

I climb over the debris: The entire forest is splattered with horse drawn wagons. Some have tumbled over, some have been damage by grenades and some are charred or totally burnt. The first one I approach is loaded with 8-centimeter grenades, the second one as well. The next contained crates with what looks like infantry ammunition for rifles and machine guns. There are also canned goods, beans and other food items. Here blacksmith tools are scattered, there is an ambulance. It must have been the ammunition unit and supply train for an entire artillery division, which was in bivouac here, caught by the bombardment of a German long distance battery.

There are coats, jackets and caps strewn around. There is a corpse. However, these are not French uniforms as known to us so far. Where have we seen before the light brown colors, the odd shaped caps, the signals on sleeves and collars before? Yes, the Polish prisoners of war, whom we have seen at home during the formation of our division, looked just like them.

We have been dealing with Polish artillery. They did survive the Polish campaign but fate caught up with them here. Hardly anyone may have escaped here. The medics had collected the wounded. The dead are covered with blankets or canvases. A man of the infantry, who thought he had found a good blanket to take along, touched a cold hand instead. His lust for booty has been cured.

Nobody had attended to the dead and wounded horses. The Poles had built temporary shelters from branches and fascines to protect them against the wind. There they lay now in long rows some on top of each other, the smooth bellies torn, the powerful sinewy limbs crushed and mangled by the hail of shrapnel of the grenades, which had exploded in the tree tops above them. Most of them are already cold and bloated. Here and there one may try to lift its head with eyes full of pain and fear. Others keep themselves upright in spite of gaping wounds, in spite of a crushed leg, and wander among the debris of the wagons and the forest riddled with shots. The staff veterinary, which had arrived at the same time at this gruesome place, shouted: "Anybody who has a heart should free the horses of their pain!" Pistol in hand we walk the rows. A shot behind the ear ends all suffering.

When I returned the flat was fixed. We quickly wash at the bunker fountain, have a few bites of bread and salami, and fill our canteens with red wine from the looted stash. Now, nothing can hold us back, although at times it is slow due to passing our oncoming units. At about 2000 hours I am able to return the motor cycle to the regiment staff at Altdorf. At about 2100 at the village road we—my operators, the French horse "Gaston" and I—are awaiting our marching battery ready to join them with our coach.

Short break by a measuring troop with the wide-angle distance
measuring instrument.

Gun leader with apprentice gunner are responsible for the accuracy and rapid fire (up to 12 rounds per minute) of the battery.

Battery troop moves into a conquered village. Pack horses for the radio equipment and telephone cable drums are led by hand.

A Maginot trench-line and pillbox with the damage of Stuka-delivered bombs.

CHAPTER 7

THE ADVANCE

Under the pressure of our attack the French retreated again during the night from their Daladier Line, the last of their fortified defense line. In front of us lies wide and open the countryside of Lorraine with its green hills, its secret deciduous forests, and uncounted villages and hamlets. Only twenty miles further south is the first of the deeply cut canyons of the four waterways: Seille, Rhine-Marne Canal, Meurthe, and Moselle. These could present difficulty and hinder our successful advance.

The general direction of the advance turns to the southwest to avoid the difficult forest and lake terrain between Dieuze and Festringen. Moerchingen and then Chateau Salins and Wisch-at-the-Seille are to be reached next. The vanguard of the division has been marching towards these destinations since the early hours of the morning.

We encountered an accident when I was trying to join my small troop with our battery advancing through Altdorf. The French horse, Gaston, is preventing us from doing so. The operators not trained in horse handling were unable to control the horse! The result was a broken wheel of our coach. What a pity. But now there is no time to be spared! The precious cargo—in addition to our equipment there are two little barrels of burgundy and a barrel of beer for the battery!—is quickly transferred to our ammunition carriers.

Under no circumstances are we to cause a slow down of the marching column! Everything continues to roll. I myself unhitched Gaston from the useless coach, buckle on stirrups, mount him in spite of his initial resistance and put into trot—a proud picture—after my battery along the marching column. From the next rest stop on he is utilized as a pole horse at the second gun.

The division marches towards Moerchingen, the battleground of the Great War. They are marching in close ranks without consideration of aircraft; the French air force is no longer a threat. The division marches without stops. The horses sweating in the noon sun are not given a minute's rest.

Several blown-up bridges are circumvented on emergency crossings. We are crossing the railroad line Metz-Strasbourg. Just outside Moerchingen, in front of the gates of a cigarette factory, girls distribute large quantities of cigarettes, the black French kind. And water as well. Greedily and noisily drink the soldiers and hurry after the column. We cannot stop, at least not before reaching the ordered village. Since this morning the division has marched for thirteen miles.

We are making our way through the narrow streets of Moerchingen. It is difficult to find the correct road. Most of the civilian did not take to flight. The women peek carefully from behind the curtains. Hardly anybody is on the street. In passing French provision storehouses are examined. There would be good additional rations—white bread, chocolate, canned fruit—in the village. If we only could rest here!

We are running into a number of farming wagons loaded high with household items, suitcases and appliances. They are evacuee farmers from Lorraine who were returning to their villages. Friendly words are exchanged between them and the marching soldiers.

After 1400 we finally reached the village designated as a resting place. A sergeant-major went ahead by bike to scout for watering possibilities and parking space. The vehicles are lined up on a meadow at the village entrance.

"Dismount! Loosen straps! Unfasten bridles! Watering!" Then the horses will have to be fed and, finally, the men receive their lunch from the field kitchen, which was over-cooked hours ago.

The two hand operated pumps of the village provide water in sparingly spurts. The electrical pumps are of no use as the cable system and power plants have been completely destroyed. Consequently, the watering is a lengthy process. And, even before all horses are satisfied, the car of the major arrives from ahead. He orders the immediate departure. So, before the soldiers and animals could satisfy their burning hunger, the unopened sacks of oats are loaded and the lid of the kettle of the field kitchen is screwed shut again.

The spearhead has made contact with the enemy! The batteries were to advance for another 4 miles and take position there. The battery troops ride off. Guns and ammunition units follow at a slower pace. Everything is being prepared for the engagement of the division. The cannons have not arrived yet. In a cherry orchard we pass the time easily.

"Eat all you can! I cannot pick the cherries up there anyway and the boys are all gone," shouted an old woman to the men, which were sitting in each one of her trees. A basket full of delicious heart cherries is quickly picked in appreciation for her friendly reception.

Just as the artillery was ready to go into position a bike messenger hurried by: "Continue on the previously designated road." It had been weak rear guards only, which gave up with hardly any fighting,

Without any further stops—we would have loved to feed the horses and have food ourselves—we marched into the evening for another four miles. Then finally we reach the resting stop anticipated by everyone. By now it is completely dark. The kettle has been emptied, although not everybody is fed. Those will have to wait for another hour. Finally, we camp a few hundred feet further along in an orchard at the southern gate of a tiny hamlet.

Today we advanced about twenty-two miles. The guns are in position in front of the camp. They are trained towards a strip of land which the French would have to pass to counter attack against our spear head during the night. Here they would be caught by our bombardment.

The horses are sleeping where they were left standing, and the soldiers where they laid down, without tents or blankets. They did not even care any longer about the barrels of beer and wine, which we brought along. A few loafs of white bread, confiscated in the village, are being cut and disappear in hungry stomachs.

The wake up call comes after a few hours of dead-to-the-world sleep. We pack and team the cannons and harness in the dark. Formation is setup again. At exactly 0500 we march.

After one hour and a half a stoppage occurs. It lasts one or two hours. From the right road endless columns of vehicles are pushing-in in front of us. This is an opportunity to fall out a little and leave the horses and vehicles in the care of a few sentries. Before we can move on, the columns coming from the right have to taper out.

Therefore, we feed and water the horses; luckily a little brook runs under the road at this point. Then the uniforms come off and into the water we go washing from head to toe. It is the first time after four days. Ah, that feels good. And then a shave! Beard off. The clean body bathes in the friendly morning sun and is dry soon. Oh Hah! The drawn out, Oh, and the shorter, Hah, of the sergeant from Hamburg sound happy and fresh and no longer fatigued and worn out. Even the hunger is forgotten, although there is no food around. The provision vehicles still have not caught up with us. Did they not keep up with us or are they lost? Now we are sitting at the rim of the road ditch writing a note to the wife, mother or bride. Who knows when and where we can post it at a flying field post office?

Aha, finally the stream of vehicles from the right is ending! The posted lookout calls. We wake our comrades sleeping on the grass. Just in time for a call coming from ahead: Get ready! A vehicle speeds up. It stops with screeching brakes. It is the major bringing new orders. For the time being no further advancement, instead encampment at the Seille and engagement of its fortifications on the opposite bank.

CHAPTER 8

IN RUBBER DINGHIES ACROSS THE SEILLE

Ordered by the major, I advance my three batteries past the little town of Chateau Salins, which was taken during the night, to a meadow just outside the village of Morville. The battery embankments are to be prepared at this vicinity. I am to continue with the observation post crew to a certain point at the adjacent ridge to receive further orders. The major and three battery commanders go ahead by car to scout for firing embankments and observation posts.

The commanding general, accompanied by his artillery commander and another general stopped his vehicle at the road crossing at Chateau Salins. A lot of gold is glistening on caps and collars. I am mounted and gallop to them and, as required, report the passing battery.

From the firing positions, the radio connection is to be established directly to the artillery operation post at the previously advised frequency. This has the highest priority. He is relying on me to see to it that the battery is ready for action on time. I repeat the order, salute and gallop after my troops.

At the firing embankments I drop off azimuth-circle information to a non-commissioned officer. He positions and prepares the battery and the signalmen build the line forward. I dispatch a courier to the rear to direct the division's quick arrival. The spotter crews and the assistant observers of the three batteries, together with the radio operators, couriers and horse handlers continue with me to ride forward.

We dismount just before the targeted hill. The horses and most of the men stay under cover. Here, protected by the hill, a multitude of vehicles of all kinds has gathered, waiting until the road clears for further advancement.

With a lieutenant and two non-commissioned officers I arrive at the designated spot.

Nobody is there. With the help of a map one more time we make sure that we are at the correct road crossings. It is correct. There is nothing else to do, but wait! From nearby bushes we can keep an eye on the crossing and also are able to scan the terrain, which is occupied by the enemy, familiarize ourselves with it and compare it to the map.

A deep valley cut across in front of us. Wooded hills are ascending over there. A side valley runs from our location point. The view to the left, where we believe the small town Wisch is located, is blocked by an outcropping height. Up there the O-posts should be established.

Several groupings of people are now hurrying up from the valley. They are not soldiers. They are carrying all sorts of things, in prams and on their backs, suitcases, bags, and boxes. The first group has reached us, inquiring excitedly whether firing is to begin. There are still many people following. They were coming from Wisch and wanted to escape to Morville before we are starting the bombardment. We learned later, that the German infantry had invaded the village early in the morning. However, they are unable to take the machine gun emplacements hiding in cellars, houses and gardens without a street-by-street fight, which would result in heavy losses. Alternatively, the division commander ordered the units to quit the village and thus cleared it up for artillery bombardment. Here, as always, the high command is trying to avoid unnecessary bloodshed. Before the evacuation the civilians have been forewarned and encouraged to find protection in cellars or even better to sit out the bombardment behind the German line.

After half an hour the division bike messenger appeared at the road crossing requesting that I accompany him to the front. The troops are to follow. I point out to the senior officer the location protected by the protruding top to the left, to which he is to lead the troops. Then we go by bike down to the valley and again up on a path through a meadow. Soon I have to dismount and scale the steep slope by foot. The driver says, "The major or captain are expecting the lieutenant over there in the direction of the out cropping.

"Not a very reliable direction," I reply anticipating some problems. However, he has no better directions.

Up we go through brush and dense young woods towards the outcropping and a lone old linden tree that protrudes from it. Naturally, I do not find anybody. An infantry captain has its operation post at the linden tree over there.

"No, we have not seen any officers of the artillery. About an hour ago there were artillerists further to the left beyond the path running on the crest of the hill, as far as I can remember even a lieutenant colonel!" Aha, the operational headquarter of the regiment! They should know the whereabouts of my major. No choice, but to look over there. My entire body is already sweating profusely, but I have to find him.

After extensive searching and repeated inquiries at the infantry, I finally arrive at the spot where the commander of the regiment had once been.

"Fifteen minutes ago," the infantry observer, who is now stationed on his own, tries to console me. "Apparently he has re-located his entrenchment further to the left."

Damn it! Back on the crest path—questioning—crossing some woods—making further inquiries—one hundred twenty feet creeping on my stomach across the enemy exposed slope of a vineyard. There I find the regimental orderly officer lying amongst the grapevines. This must be it.

"Are you, Lieutenant Colonel, in contact with the IV Division?"

"Well, I hoped to learn from you their whereabouts."

"Continue your urgent search. The division should contact us immediately. In about an hour we are to commence firing."

I am absolutely drenched with sweat. Once again I run to the outcropping. Nobody is there. Therefore, we have to establish our own O-post. We move down to the rendezvous point, where the battery troops have arrived in the meantime.

"Pick-up your equipment and follow," I order them. No sooner do we climb the slope again. I am reaching nearly the end of my strengths. During the past day and a half I had only two slices of white bread and a handful of cherries. The radioman with his backpack equipment and the assistant observer with the stereo-telescope are panting behind me. If necessary we shall establish our own O-post, if possible close to the operational entrenchment enabling us to receive the firing orders directly.

We are coming to the cross path. A captain is finally meeting us and we both are relieved. He has the firing order.

At exactly 1500 hours it is to start. Prior to this the guns have to be battered down and firing orders prepared for four targets. The captain, being the acting major, cannot assist me. I look at my watch: it is 1440. We just should be able to manage. Quickly we cross the stand of woods at the edge of the vineyard.

"Set-up radio equipment here. Establish connection to the operational post. Obtain the coordinates and base direction of the batteries! The others form a chain of dispatchers to me," I order. I grab the firing order pouch and crawl onto the vineyard. One hundred twenty more feet and I should have a clear view.

In front of me in the valley is the village of Wisch. Deep heavy thunderclouds hang over it. Running the valley is the silvery ribbon of the Seille River. It intersects the village.

It is 1447 hours. I take the map board and transfer onto the map the target points requested by the chief. The coordinates and base direction of the batteries are verbally transmitted to me. The signalmen have established contact and the communication by mouth functions as well in spite of the heavy gusts of wind, which were now preceding the thunderstorm.

I am drawing on the map the emplacement and base direction and pin above it the clinometers. With this makeshift arrangement, I am able to measure the distance of the various targets. Curse it, the rain is now pouring down. The firing will even be more inaccurate due to the wet map.

I am ready with one target. I shout it to the first man of the dispatcher chain, who runs off in the sheets of water.

"Firing order: Third charge, impact, entire battery! From base 10 more! (This indicates the side deviation); Forty-two hundred (This represents the distance to the target); Spirit level 290 (Since the target lies below the battery); one group!" My batteries are ready.

At 1456 hours I hear the sound of four shots. It is four minutes before the general bombardments start. Thanks to St. Barbara the grenades are more or less on target and no further adjustments are necessary! The firing plans had been very, very rudimentary. The four grenades are now whistling way above us. And there, these are the smoke clouds of the hits. One, two, three and there the fourth. St. Barbara did help. At the right edge of the village the bombardment is still a little too far, but not by much.

"Thirty more! Same distance! One group!" I am shouting a correction for the left. It is 1500 and I give the order: "Fire!"

The artillery roars and launch their shells. Again there is whistling overhead from the long range guns in the rear. Explosions and gray clouds erupt among the back rows of Wisch's houses.

The captain and temporary division commander is crouched left of me in the vineyard at the stereo-telescope. I report to him: "Battering down completed!" At the same time we are receiving by wire the order to commence bombardment on target 303. I order through the dispatchers and walking box pattern: my batteries would fire a perimeter while others walked up and down this box, systematically destroying anything within it.

During the bombardment the rain pours down. Without a coat or rain gear, we are soaked to the skin within seconds. Entire streams of cold water are running down our backs through the collar. I have to close the map board to prevent the plan from completely disintegrating. The field glasses are fogged up from the water. We have to watch by naked eye. However, we are able to identify our hits from the numerous smoke clouds rising from all parts of the village. In addition to us only light batteries are firing. The other heavy batteries of our division were not as fortunate. They were not ready.

From the operational center we are now receiving the order: "Advance firing line! Our own infantry is attacking!" They are already advancing there to the left. They literally are flying down the slope. Once they are running and jumping they are unable to stop again on the slippery ground of loam.

Once at the bottom they carry rubber dinghies across the free strip of grass along the river. Guns still fire across the river from the enemy-held bank. However, the speed of the attack is not to be stopped. The storm battalion is mainly comprised of men of the S.A. regiment "Feldherrnhalle." They reach the banks simultaneously at three spots. Into the water go the boats. They rapidly paddle to the other side, land and are dispersing through the meadows. They have now reached the protection of the gardens and the bushes. The French seem to have run.

The resistance has been broken. At the other side of town the same thing must have happened. No longer are there any shots or hand grenade explosions to be heard.

The rain stopped as suddenly as it came. The regiment commander let it be known that only, "the 3rd battery will fire upon request and agreement." That means that we have again to get in touch with the infantry. I collect my things and retreat across the vineyard. The men of the dispatch chain and the radio operator are happy. They all have the feeling everything went well, very well, in spite of the bad weather and the enormous speed. Everybody prides himself on having made a contribution.

"That worked out well lieutenant," offered non-commissioned officer Klaus with a grin.

"Yes, Klaus that it has. But now pay attention. You see down there the three crossing points. As soon as they have dismantled their equipment follow me on the double with the signalmen to the middle crossing. I shall go ahead and find the battalion commander. Bring signalmen to the third crossing, lieutenant, but on the double!"

"This will be done, I can rely on it," he repeats with another grin.

And it was done. At the crossing I posted an infantryman to lead Klaus and the signalman forward to the temporary battalion destination, which I had located in the meantime. They joined up with me at the battalion commander at the fork of the road on the other side of the woods. And quickly they established a connection to the firing positions. However, further firing orders were not necessary, only the position. For the time being there was no resistance and the infantry would still advance further than the next village, Arracourt.

From below they transmitted an important message: France had inquired about the terms of a possible armistice. We requested confirmation of the message. It was correct. There was great rejoicing, initially at the battalion's operation post, where I read the message aloud and from there it ran like a wild fire along the entire line. Everything went out of control. All acted contrary to all rules and fighting regulations. Loud shouts of joy were around us. We saw men nearby breaking out in dances of joy. And at dusk the evening sky along the front line was filled with fireworks of white flares.

We were positioned exactly near the old border between France and Alsace-Lorraine. Where will be the new border of the Reich? In a happy mood new borders were drawn, colonies re-distributed and reparation payments levied. Then the captain, my former revered battery chief, who volunteered to lead a storm company, joined us. Many stories were exchanged. There was victorious jubilation in the air. Here, at the spear-head of a division pushing into France, we forgot for fifteen minutes that there is still a war going on. Over there, maybe in the next village, French machineguns are waiting for us. If we really wanted to destroy the army retreating before us we still had ahead of us a number of exhausting marching and fighting days.

We have to be on our way. The infantry advances further to the next village. With the signalmen I march back to find the battery. When we enter Wisch, the dead are still lying in the streets; some of them are terribly maimed. But there is again lively activity. The civilians who had fled are returning in large groups. Everything is being cleaned up. On the main street there is surprisingly little left to see of the bombardment. Some stores are open again. Citizens and also some German soldiers are shopping. I find at a jeweler a pretty silver bracelet with a charm of Lorraine. A greeting to be sent home.

The first vehicles are now moving over the blown up bridge, which has received emergency repairs by the engineering corps. There are light guns, armored vehicles, anti-tank cannons, and heavy machine guns; also trucks with ammunition and sapper equipment. On the other side of the bridge I catch a motor bike, which quickly takes me back and close to the firing post. I report to the battery chief shortly before midnight.

And then a visit to the field kitchen! The cook is filling my tin plate over and over gain with heavy lentils. He is smiling happily about the obvious appreciation of his art. But then again during the last two days I hardly had a few bites. Further more it happens to be my favorite dish.

Non-commissioned officer Klaus returned as well. He had met me with the signalmen at the front. On their way they came across seven scattered Frenchmen in the gardens of Wisch. Klaus arrested them and utilized them immediately to take back the wounded. The medics would have been unable to manage on their own.

The guns have been removed from the embankments and have been readied from transport up to assure an early departure in the morning and crossing of the Seille River without delay.

Thirty minutes after midnight we crawl into the straw of a barn to quickly catch two hours of sleep.

CHAPTER 9

AGAINST THE CANAL FORTIFICATIONS

Roll call is at 0230 hours, departure in deep darkness at 0300 hours. We are advancing on the same road, which I had taken back over the Seille last night. Out of the dark a voice inquires: "Is this the 11th Battery?"

The advance continues. At dawn we have reached Wisch at the Seille.

On a hill to the right of the road are two fresh soldiers' graves within the shade of an ancient oak. The first rays of the morning sun fall on the light wooden crosses with helmets on them. Pink and red roses have been strewn on the mounts.

Here lies Major M., commander of the 3rd Battalion, and next to him, his driver. During the past days, I have run into him over and over again at the head of the advancing infantry. His light division was always the first ready to fire behind the infantry thus helping the forward moving attack. Early yesterday morning he was also one of the first at the village perimeter when the vanguard troops entered Wisch, which was still occupied by the enemies. They allowed him to come very close and shot him down through the head, him and his driver. Now they are resting in the hollowed ground of Lorainne.

Last night I spoke briefly with his battery chief who had been sitting next to him. A bullet hit him through his collar as well and a second through his right boot behind the calf. By now he and his battery are again way in front.

We are now passing the first houses of town to the river and the foot of the bridge. The main girder of the bridge is broken across the middle and collapsed. The relatively undamaged roadways are precipitously leading down into the river on one side and up from the river on the other. A sturdy wood construction built by the engineer corps bridges the gap on the bottom. Vehicle after vehicle, one at a time, pass over this difficult spot. They approach quickly and go down, with buoyancy they go up on the other side. If a vehicle gets stuck on the steep roadway, a team of helpers stands by ready to push. Riders dismount and lead their horses across. At the approach the general of the division himself makes sure that there are no blockages and delays. Today this represents the bottleneck, the most difficult spot that will influence the speed of our advance.

The convoys are moving forward in close formation. For the time being they are still on the same road on which I marched back last night when returning from the storm battalion. Then we pass through Arracourt, a clean village with large prosperous looking farms. It marks the French frontier before the 1918 demarcation annexed Alsace Lorraine.

Now comes a new engagement! This time it is against the fortifications of the Rhine-Marne Canal. The battle noise seems to indicate heavy fighting at the front lines.

I am leading my battery, trotting forward to the point where the road leaves the protection of a wooded hill and turns sharply to the left. The terrain in front of us is under enemy bombardment. The ordinances are exploding, mostly a few at the same spot, first here at the stand of trees to the left, than over there at the exit of the village, and than again on the height to the right of us. It is just a question of time, until this important fork in the road, to which we were ordered, will get its share. But the observation crew has to stay close by. Therefore, the horses are led back here to the open meadow—we no longer have to worry about planes—though the men with their horses are scattered as far apart as possible.

The placement has been satisfactorily completed. We are awaiting orders. There is another salvo coming. It was directed toward the street and us. Everyone not holding a horse dives into the ditch of the road. Four hits explode. One appears to be to the right, dangerously close to the horses. Lifting my head I am looking over there. For heaven's sake, my orderly with his and my horse lies on the ground. Somebody is running towards him when he rises and looks around him in a daze. Then my horse gets up and the other horse too is struggling to rise. All three were on their legs before we could reach them.

They had been thrown down by the blast of the exploding ordinance. We examined the horses. Mine had been scratched on the right hind leg by small shrapnel. However, it bled quite profusely even through the emergency bandage of white rags. Otherwise everything is in order. A week later my stead Pirol is able to carry me again. But he did not look well and was slightly sick for a long time, most likely due to the loss of blood.

On the heights behind us to the right, batteries are taking positions everywhere, light field mortars, long barrel guns and heavy motorized units. The regimental commander is advancing in his field vehicle. The observers are climbing up the hill.

I cannot stand it any longer. I cannot wait until I am picked up. The battery has to be ready for firing as soon as possible. Looking at the map and the terrain before of me, I order the non-commissioned officer: "You and the O-crew stay here until you are collected by the chief. I will advance with the signalmen to the other side of the stand of woods there in front of this hill and command the battery from there."

Half an hour later we hide at the top, field glasses are pressed to my face. We are at the edge of the dense forest-like bushes, the signalmen is behind me. On our way up I ran into the commander of the regiment and received the outline of the area under our watch and the target allocations. I am surveying the occupied enemy terrain before me. The view into the deep valley of Sanon, through which the Rhine-Marne Canal runs, is very limited. However, the opposite heights are in clear view. A number of church steeples indicate the position of the villages surrounding them. I am picking one about in the middle of our target area. In its direction I shall land the battery with high exploding ordinances.

The signalmen have established contact and receive the position and level of the battery. Now I can prepare the firing order. The lead gun fires towards the church steeple selected by me with a timing ordinance. Before the ordinance hits the ground, it explodes high in the air. The white smoke vanes of the detonators hover above the church spire. After a few corrections they are in the exact direction right above it.

The level of the battery has been checked. The bombardment of the blind spot in the valley, determined by the commander, can commence. I have the target transmitted back to the arithmeticians. They have to calculate exactly the deviation of the new direction from the church tower just fired upon. I am unable to see the new target and cannot make any correction to the shots by observation. As we found out later from the infantry and from our own investigation at location, the bombardment, however, were right on target and was very effective.

As suitable as our present location may be for an observation post, it had one disadvantage: three to six hundred feet in front of us are several groupings of bushes in which three other batteries have established their O-posts. All the traffic to them, especially the cable-laying signal troupe, has to pass us nearby. My efforts to have the runners, signalmen etc. move under protection were in vain. Over and over again one or two men appear upright and clearly visible from the brush next to us. There will be consequences for their stupidity! Sure enough, while still securing the battery, the French had enough and dispatched a few medium size ordinances in our direction. The next hits are even closer behind us in the bushes. Shrapnel is whistling and humming above us and leaves and branches rain down while we are lying flat in small ground indentations. From here on they do not leave us in peace. Over and over again we have to bury our noses in the dirt, before we were able to transmit our instructions.

Apparently, it was possible to see the French bombardment of our position and the chief must have contacted an O-post less exposed. In any event the signalman picked-up the following order: "Advance spotter to retreat immediately to street fork 2 ½ miles south of Arracourt."

When we arrive at the fork sweating, the bike driver is waiting. Soon the entire battery troop is reunited in a new observing post; a deep hole behind a steep wall. Regardless of the intensity of the French bombardment unless it is a direct hit nothing can happen to us here,.

All afternoon the bombardment is heavy. The gray clouds of dirt and smoke rise uninterrupted amongst the infantry, which we can see lying in front of us in quickly dug holes. The batteries are positioned in front of us. The ground is quivering. Once in a while a lump of dirt or stone flies into our hole. The advance spotter of the neighboring battery is brought back with shrapnel in his leg. The motorized long barrel cannons assigned to us suffer heavy damage. One cannon has been turned over by a direct hit, completely twisted and full of holes. Now a grenade explodes exactly at the spot where the second troop leader was just standing. Nothing remains of him.

We, however, sit safely behind our wall and are surveying by stereo-telescope the heights of the other canal embankment. There is some movement, especially within the section of the left neighboring division. We can see the French leading column after column over the forested heights down to the canal. First we noted them in the distance coming from the forest down the road from left to right behind the village with the strangely pointed spire. Then they appear again at the forward village exit, much closer than before. Marching and driving from right to left they are going up the road until they disappear again on the densely forested height. There in the woods they seem to get ready for engagement or to entrench for defense. A few advanced patrols and cyclers even emerge further in front and quite close to the canal.

Not only are the infantry columns moving this way, but also bicycle units, and numerous horse drawn vehicles like anti-tank cannon, heavy machine guns and field artillery. Anxiously we are watching the build up for several hours.

Despite the excellent targets, we are ordered to hold our fire. The heart of the artillerist bleeds! The battery is then needed for targets further right of our own section. At the infantry's request we are firing on calculated targets.

Thus we are limited to only transmit continuously our observations to the high command via our operational post. We see the result of the requested harassing fire with columns of smoke which rise scattered above the forest from time to time.

Apparently, under pressure at the sections on both their sides, during the night the phantom enemy moved again, but in the opposite direction. In the morning, when our infantry occupied the opposite heights, only a few remainders—deserted vehicles, ammunition and armament items—bore witness to yesterday's build up.

Towards evening the enemy fire stopped. The resistance may have again been broken. The French artillery is again repositioning by going backwards.

The battery chief returns to the firing embankment with a few men. With the remainder of the O-crew I am setting up a tent at our location. Then we finally receive provisions and mail, for the first time since the advance, letters and parcels from home.

At desert we have fresh milk. The communication platoon leader, a farmer in peace time, was able to milk one of the free running cows after a long chase.

Together we are enjoying the evening in peace. Everyone is spooning out of his kit, reading his letters or, in between, digging into a parcel. The hot day is forgotten, forgotten are weariness and hunger, forgotten the noise of the hits and the drone of the shots.

We sleep deeply and dreamlessly, a full night for the first time in days. Outside the tents the guard listens into the still bright night to the occasional shot and the rattle of the machine guns, a reminder of the fighting vanguards way in front across the canal.

CHAPTER 10

CROSSING THE MEURTHE RIVER

I am with the division commander at dawn. Frozen and tired he crawls out of his hole in the ground, the staff officers did not fare any better. They did not sleep under the protection of a tent as we did. A canteen of red burgundy, circulating from mouth-to-mouth, soon revived everybody quickly.

No battle noises can be heard from the front. Apparently the French retreated again during the night from the positions they were holding yesterday. Today the advance will be fast. These are assumptions, which quickly have to be confirmed. I am immediately to go ahead as the artillery liaison of the division, connect with the infantry and report back to the officer in charge as soon as possible for him to advance the batteries if necessary.

I go back to the O-post to put the non-commissioned officer in charge and to inform him about my mission. In the meantime the signalmen are packed. We march in a hurry into the dewy morning. Everybody is breaking camp. Observation posts of light batteries, emplacements of infantry cannons and heavy machine guns are dismantled or are already on the move.

In yesterday's hard fought village I meet up with the reserve company of the storm battalion, just as it got ready to follow it. The company leader had received the latest news from the front and from the neighboring units.

Only a flat ridge is separating us from the Rhine-Marne Canal and the Sanon Valley beyond. On the top I have the wireless equipment installed. From here I can overlook the hilly terrain on the other side, which is now quickly ascended by our infantry units.

Further to the right are the heights of Virtimont. At this location the attack of the German regiments was stopped in 1914. The foremost and highest of the hills is crowned with an erected stone, a memorial to the 11th French Division, which defended the position heroically at that time.

Again this is the decisive battle for the canal fortifications. Last night the battalions moving from the right and the left have taken the high elevations in quick attacks, while the village in front of them was still being fought over. It was all accomplished in less than two hours. The coordination with the advanced storm infantry and the artillery was excellent. They drove up in full view of the enemy and eliminated the machine gun and mortar pillboxes quickly from an unprotected firing position. The success should earn the battalion commander the knight-cross for his inspiring personal initiative, which started the attack rolling before friend or enemy expected it.

We hear two muffled explosions and black columns of smoke rise high at the horizon. The French are blowing up the bridges after their retreat over the next river, the Meurthe.

The radio connection has been established. I can report to the rear: "Neighboring regiments have reached both sides of the Meurthe. At our own section the infantry has crossed the canal and advancing towards Luneville, Deuxville and the Meurthe River. At about 2000 two large blasts have occurred, presumably of bridges over the Meurthe. From the current position the division can no longer reach the enemy. I am proceeding forward and will rejoin the division at Deuxville."

Beside us on the heights stand anti-aircraft cannon providing a firing screen for the infantry. While the signalmen are setting up their equipment, the gunner conveys to me an event, similar to the one I heard with horror circulating already yesterday. An exhausted man of his company slept for a few hours in the barn of a lonely farm. He disregarded all caution due to his weariness. He must have been assaulted in the morning and both his eyes were gorged. He, the gunner, had seen the poor comrade personally. None of the eight inhabitants of the farm survived. They all were shot.

Luckily, this was the only case of atrocities committed by civilians during the entire campaign, which could be confirmed to me beyond the shadow of a doubt.

The signalmen are ready. On the road to Luneville we are stopping the communication vehicle of the regiment headquarters. It takes us along via an emergency bridge over the canal, leaving the town Einville to the right and turning further to the Southwest.

The highway to Luneville goes straight to the south. On both sides of the road, one company of our infantry regiment is hurriedly advancing. Where are they going? In accordance with the last order from headquarters the direction for our engagement is much further to the right. The town of Luneville falls within the sector of the neighboring division to the left. I cannot catch them any more and the regimental car has to go ahead urgently further to the right. So, they are keeping the attack direction towards Luneville.

I learn later that the new orders had never reached the two companies. In accordance with the previous order they occupied Luneville, a town of 25,000, on their own, way ahead of the front, two hours prior to arrival of the neighboring division, which was in charge.

Finally, I have them drop my signalmen and myself at the north entrance of the village, Deuxville, to wait for our division commander.

We are now in an area that the German army never reached in WWI. The area had served as a French frontal communication zone and was only in reach of German artillery.

The signalmen set up the equipment, but cannot get a connection. That indicated that the battery is on its way. We have lots of time until it catches up with us. There is time for washing in the village brook, to shave and to have breakfast from the rations.

The women in the doorways look at us with fright. It is difficult to calm them and only slowly they open up. But they finally talk. They said that only during the night the French retreated after billeting here uninterrupted for nearly a year. Have the French soldiers trained a lot?

"Mais non! They never trained. They slept only and ate, they ate very well." They did not even take good care of the horses. They just threw the oats on the floor and that not every day."

"And what was the reaction of the officers?" I asked as best I could.

"Oh, the officers! They stayed from Friday to Monday at Nancy. On other days, they did not have much of a presence either. The never looked into the barns or at the horses."

We begin to understand. The old fighting spirit of the honored French armies, which still existed at the beginning of the war, slowly and quietly disappeared during the long winter billeting.

We were surprised that many farms were deserted, although the animals stood in the barns and some signs indicated that they were taken care of a little while ago.

"Yes, most of them left in a hurry," we are being told. When they heard "the Germans are coming" the whole village was stricken with wild fear. The women grabbed a few things, mostly unimportant stuff, took their children and took off, aimlessly and thoughtless, as long as it was away from the "Hun." Earlier all young men had been forced to "evacuate". The few elders, who remained calm, could not influence the excited women. The effects of the gruesome stories repeated for decades of cut-off hands, murdered women and butchered children were still too strong. There had been numerous refugees in the village, which had come from locations next to the German border and had been in constant contact with the neighboring German villages as part of the border traffic. They too were overcome by the fear-psychosis and fled, although they must have known the Germans as decent and peace loving people! How much greater must the effect of these gruesome fairy tales be on the French population in the center of the country.

Several automobiles have been left behind by civilians, who had fled, and by the army. These vehicles are searched out immediately. Tempted by the many small advantages and comforts both while serving and while off duty, every horse-drawn unit dreams of acquiring as many motor-driven vehicles as possible. Consequently, everybody with time on his hands is trying to find abandon vehicles for his unit—in most cases without success. Either an essential part is missing completely—starter, battery or accelerator—or the vehicle will not start in spite of tireless cranking and pushing due to an unknown internal defect.

I participate as well with eagerness and with the loss of plenty of sweat in these attempts of healing and repairing. Unfortunately, also without real success. In the end my signalmen locate in a garage a nearly brand new four seat Peugeot. The owner, however, had stayed. With shaking hands she is handing over the keys. Our battery was in great need of a new vehicle for the chief, since the motorbike has been on its last leg for days. I request permission from the major, who just had arrived in his vehicle ahead of his division, to requisition the Peugeot for "important military purposes." The owner was happy to receive a written confirmation, which would assure her re-imbursement of the value of the vehicle at a later date.

Quickly we load the signalmen and their equipment. At the steering wheel of the automobile I am following the major scouting the new engagement.

The River Meurthe runs in a bend of about six miles diameter towards the north and just west of Luneville. At the villages on the southern part of the curve the French dug in one more time on their bank. But tonight they were to be forced out of these positions. In preparation of the attack our division has the order to fire.

We find suitable firing locations in the forest about two miles from the Meurthe. With the soon arriving battery troop I continue to ride forward through the woods close to the river. It is a wonderful ride with the afternoon sun beaming through the young stands of fir and beech trees.

Between the woods and the river is a suburban development. We leave the horses behind in the forest and advance from house to house, always protected from the enemy who is lying just a few hundred feet in front of us. We stop at a high placed house that promised a good view of the opposite river bank. The stereo-telescope is installed right under the roof in the attic. A few roofing tiles are pushed aside for an undisturbed telescope view over the villages and heights on the other side. Quickly I compare terrain and map aided by the stereo-telescope. Straight ahead and to the middle of the right are the two villages that are targeted for our initial bombardment. We are ready!

However, we are not yet in contact with the battery. The two signalmen crews, who have started laying the cable from both sides simultaneously, apparently have not yet met in the middle. Luckily, the second connection, the wireless transmitter, is now operative. This has to do initially, although the communication is not very good.

The battery reports its readiness. A few battering down shots towards the church tower over there, confirm that the battery is trained properly.

At exactly 2000 hours the bombardment of the villages, occupied by the enemy, begins. Some fires can be seen. The villages are soon enveloped in smoke. It is time for the infantry attack. The bombardment stops abruptly. From our position we are unable to see the river and the place of crossing. However, everything seems to go as planned. On the other side a white flare shoots up—the sign of the infantry: "We are here!" And in no time flares are following from where one would imagine the edge of the villages and the heights ascending behind it. The attack has been successful. For us the expected marching orders will end a short night.

But first we have time to think of bodily libations. The provision supply line, however, has not caught up with us. Instead my men have reconnoitered a provision wholesaler or something similarly pleasant. They find mostly sweets. We are satisfying the hunger pains with canned fruit and delicious cookies, which we find in uncountable high stacked tins. We quench our thirst with selected red wines. Under the light of the stars and the shine of the still burning fires on the other side, we picked in the garden the first ripe red currants.

After an hour's sleep on garden chairs, couches and beds the shrill alarm sounds. We depart for the crossing of the Meurthe. We are not crossing here, but we have to go to the far right to find the now usable emergency bridge.

On the side-car bike I accompany the chief to the firing embankment. There I am ordered by the commander to find and direct all units of the division that still have not gathered at the collection point in the pitch-dark night and the endless forest. I mount the tireless horse of the chief—my faithful horse is still suffering from injuries received the day before yesterday—and ride into the forest hoping that I shall meet somewhere in the dark the missing vehicles and soldiers on the way to the O-posts.

Against all expectations it went well. After a few minutes at the edge of the path I find the first of the three missing communication vehicles. The other two, close together in the middle of the forest, are found after another fifteen minutes. The loud conversation of the men, which was contrary to all regulations, pointed me to their direction. I give the drivers exact direction to the bridge so that they cannot get lost again. There they will be able to connect with the division as the crossing always results in delays. I also give direction to a lost battery unit. From soldiers of other units I learn that the missing regimental communication unit has passed here on its way to the bridge. Finally, I find my own O-troop a bit further down at the edge of the woods.

The ride through the night was with some romantic allurements—to the right the high dark forest of Vitrimont, to the left the burning villages on the left bank of the Meurthe. The blaze leads us in about two hours to the emergency bridge. The engineer corps had erected it during the night next to the destroyed stone bridge.

At dawn our division is the first unit to cross. I can report to the commander that all vehicles and troops have joined on time.

Once across the river and after a short march the division rests in a meadow to await orders. The horses drink and feed. They stand sleepy and drowsy, tired and indifferent. We all wash thoroughly in the brook and have a hardy breakfast out of all sorts of cans that were requisitioned yesterday by the ammunition unit at a factory along the route. Then we too are stretching out in the grass for a short nap.

CHAPTER 11

A DIVISION SURRENDERS

At about 9 o'clock we receive the new order, "Fast advance to the South." The next seven villages along the road are listed by name. First marching destination is the town of Charmes-at-the-Moselle, about eighteen miles from here.

Today we can progress fast on the road. Our battery is marching at the head of the division. There are also no other convoys directly in front of us. This eliminates the frequent delays, those repeating short hold ups with stopping and dismounting, with getting ready, mounting and starting up, all of which are more tiring for men and horses than a quick and uninterrupted march.

Towards midday, however, we are delayed for a longer time. An infantry division advancing on the same road has missed the ordered direction, "gotten off course." It had to turn back and is now re-entering the correct road in front of us. This break forced on us is an opportunity to feed and water our exhausted horses in the sun.

It becomes quite apparent that we are on the heels of the French. Their previously orderly retreats have changed to flight. On both sides of the road are long rows of armaments and equipment discarded by the retreating companies. Knapsacks and coats, haversacks, canteens, and harnesses are piled up. All items not essential for battle. However, in between there are more and more weapons of all sorts, helmets and rifles, pistols, bayonets, hand grenades, and infantry ammunition; all items that a soldier only gives up when he believes everything is lost.

Even the officers seem to have panicked. We find officers' belts and coats, field glasses, map containers, and pistols. At the curb the passing men pick up a few souvenirs. Abandoned guns, ditched vehicles and a few shot horses at the edge of the road indicate that their artillery did not have time for an orderly retreat either.

It is important now that the pursuit not slow down. The enemy ahead of us has to be marched into its death! They should not have another opportunity to position their guns, to distribute new ammunition, to collect their soldiers, and to re-group for defense. We all are aware of it. Nobody thinks of resting in spite of the exertion during the last six days, in spite of the depressing heat, in spite of the choking dust, in spite of the extreme weariness. I watch riders on horses fall asleep again and again.

The horses too are at their end. For six days and nights they were harnessed. They hardly had one night of proper rest. They had to pull and pull the heavy guns and the overloaded wagons, every day for 30 miles and more, up long and steep slopes, crossing bumpy emergency bridges and difficult detours. And with all of this, they never were properly fed. They were watered and fed quite infrequently, depending on opportunities, and often at much to long intervals. We treat our four legged comrades with as much indulgence as possible. We marched long distance by foot, the riders next to their horses, and the gunners behind their guns. We utilized every possibility of marching hold ups and rests to water them or let them graze at the edge of the road. The weakest of them we unharnessed and exchanged for fresh captured horses. But in spite of all these measures they are at the end of their strength. Their hanging heads, their cloudy eyes, and their hollow sides is a clear indication of their exhaustion.

After a long hot marching day we arrive in the late afternoon near the nine miles long and 5 miles deep forest of Charmes, which is situated in front of the Moselle. It appears the enemy has dug in for a last desperate stand. We hear infantry firing and our advance artillery is also participating in the fight, judging from the drone of the shots to the right and left.

Our division too is taking up one more time a firing position. The guns are moving up on a bumpy steep rising hill. The gunners are getting ready to fire—it would be for the last time in this campaign. Besides the batteries calculators are already at work. No observation posts are established so, apparently, firing by map only is being considered.

I am ordered by the major to go ahead into the forest as liaison officer to the infantry headquarters. I should direct as its forward observer the fire of my battery. Great caution has to be exercised with the shelling of the enemy's hinterlands since near Verdun and Toul the advancing German motorized divisions may be very close.

With some difficulties I am able to locate within the long convoys the radio car of the signal unit. From the battery chief I request the automobile newly captured at Deuxville. I am loading the division radioman, my own battery operator and their equipment. Then we speed forward into the night.

We pass through a village located in front of the forest on a commanding hill. A lonely farm stays to the left. I know it houses the operation posts of the regiment commander and the major. Then we submerge into the forest of Charmes. The road leads into it straight as an arrow as far as we can see.

What might the situation be at the end of the forest? Returning officers indicate that the infantry headquarters I am looking for has been advanced to the other edge of the forest just a few hundred feet from the Moselle. Apparently there had been surrender negotiations with the division in front of us. But during the late afternoon another enemy division launched a relief attack with numerous tanks, which in the fighting within the woods caused great losses to our advanced infantry. Another artillery officer told me that a friend of his, a 1st lieutenant, and his O-crew were missing. With a handful of volunteers he was searching for him. Unfortunately, I cannot join them since my orders call for a different direction.

As we find out later, the 1st lieutenant and his men were indeed cut off during the relief attack and taken as prisoners. A French sharp shooter company took them along. When later on they were engaged at another point with German advance troops, the 1st lieutenant beseeched the French company leader about the hopelessness of the situation to such an extent that he wavered whether to continue the fight. The German prisoners took advantage of this moment of hesitation: they grabbed the weapons from their guards and in turn ordered them to surrender. They brought the entire company back as prisoners!

We drive further into the forest. Ahead we can hear some shooting. In ditches to the right and left of the road we recognize the silhouettes of wagons and automobiles. Horses are roaming around. We are running into larger groups of prisoners. The end really seems to be coming for the French.

I make a note of my observations and send it back by car from about the middle of the forest. With the signalmen I march on by foot for half an hour.

To the left of the road, I finally find on top of a shot up armored vehicle an infantry colonel and with him the battalion commander of a second infantry regiment. I report to him as the artillery liaison officer. They request my major and also my regiment commander to join them as quickly as possible. The division should be trained on the village between the Moselle and the railroad. Enemy resistance might still be possible there. The French division general has just surrendered after he had been released back to his units this afternoon on his word of honor. By dropping a message a reconnaissance plane of a panzer division reported at 1900 hours the approach of the surrendering enemy division from the south. However, it is wise to be prepared for the worst.

How can we convey this information to the rear? The wireless operators have set up their equipment and are constantly calling the corresponding stations. However, neither division operational headquarters nor my battery is responding. The distance seems to be too great for our equipment, especially within the forest.

I am useless here without contact to the rear. The information has to go back. I jump on the back seat of a motorbike, which is just departing to the rear as guard to the captured French general.

The forest falls quickly behind and I find the operational posts after extensive searching in the pitch dark night. I personally deliver the message and direct on the map the driver and signalman in charge of laying the cable. After I spoke by radio with the battery chief as well, I find a bundle of straw under the stars and rested for two hours.

The next morning everything is over. The enemy is no longer fighting. At dawn I return again by foot to the front to join my wireless operators and to hopefully capture a truck for the battery. Along the entire perimeter of the woods white rags flutter on makeshift poles: the sign of surrender. A deserted battery stands not far from the road at the perimeter of the forest. The French gunners have dropped the long barrels from the gun carriages to render them temporarily unusable. Behind it in the woods are a lot of dead horses. Yesterday our long barrel guns reached here.

On the road the countless prisoners in their long coats march in columns of three and move towards me in a continuous flow. Among them are long convoys of captured horse-drawn vehicles, entire supply companies, medical units, and ammunition trains. The French drivers and brake men are still sitting on the lead horses and coach boxes. Judging from their happy faces they have no objection to the reversal of the marching direction.

At the perimeter of the road are virtual mountains of tinny French helmets, in between knapsacks, belts, rifles and gas masks with their long hoses. In the ditches are turned over trucks, guns, campaign cars. Where the truck walls had collapsed the contents often was scattered on the road. Here is a sack of sugar next to cases of delicate cold cuts in tins, there is a stack of jackets and riding britches. There are even partial and full cases from a medical unit. And here is freshly roasted coffee heaped up in the ditch. I take off my helmet and fill it. This will make a nice parcel from the battlefield to back home!

When I step to the side of the road into the thick brush I always find groups of deserted horses grazing on leaves and forest herbs. Looking down towards the crossroads, the way is packed full of vehicles, especially trucks of all sorts and sizes with guns, tanks and automobiles scattered in between.

A whole division is in the forest. The prisoners—in large and small groups—are appearing now and fall into the columns, which are marching to the assembly camp at the rear. Our division alone is sending back nearly sixteen thousand prisoners.

A week of strenuous work is ahead of us: all deserted horses must be assembled, the countless equipment and material can be gathered, inspected and counted. The division collected two thousand captured horses. At the collection center they counted twenty-five thousand helmets, the same number of gas masks, eighteen thousand rifles, one thousand four hundred machine guns, and nearly three hundred guns. Among the three thousand cars and trucks at the parking lot, sixty-five are armored vehicles.

The three wireless operators at the edge of the forest welcome me back happily and impatiently: "Lieutenant! Ahead to the left in the forest are trucks ready to be driven, there are at least ten in one location! But other soldiers are looking at them too. The lieutenant has to come immediately."

Yesterday our only truck caught fire from a nearby exploding howitzer shell and completely burnt. Without a truck, however, a battery is impeded. Any self-assistance for re-supply and securing of provisions, as required in unfriendly territory, is paralyzed.

Let's go!—Quickly to the parking lot in the forest! A ha, there are the trucks, driven wildly in between the trees. It must be the convoy of a headquarters unit, maybe a divisional headquarters. The numerous officers' luggage and orderly cases full of papers indicate it. Infantry and storm troops are in the process of reviewing the cases and suitcases and to secure important files, paper and other items. Especially desirable are French pistols and field glasses.

I am more interested in the trucks. I check them out carefully, one after the other, the motors, and the year of make, capacity, tires and gasoline level. Nearly all of the heavy trucks are useless. I am opting for the 1 ½ ton truck. But how can I get it out? Four other vehicles are standing in all directions in front of it. Its own steering wheel points into the forest. The ground is soggy and soft.

Four yellow-striped signalmen are working on the neighboring vehicle. They have the same problem as we have.

"Come on, comrades! Give us a hand. We will help each other!" This way we make quick progress. Heavily loaded trucks are pushed aside by combined men power. Boxes and crates are moved out of the way, a few little trees cut down and their branches laid down to make a firm track. Now we can try it! Slowly I reverse onto the branches. My corporal standing behind the vehicle waves directions to me. Spinning—then I am stuck. One more tree has to be felled. After two more forward and reverse attempts our truck stands free on the road.

We free the second vehicle quickly and assign it to the signalmen. We have done it! But we all sweat profusely. In the meantime the sun stands high, nearly due south. There is a happy surprise. We find a stack of brown French military shirts, just enough for all of us. We finally can shed the sweaty and dusty shirts worn during the advance. The bodies are washed with soap in the spring fed brook down there and dressed with pleasure in the clean laundry. Wonderful!

In the best mood we are driving our truck along the still marching columns of prisoners to the firing embankment of the battery. There we hand over our find under the welcome of our comrades.

CHAPTER 12

VICTORY

Everybody at the embankment is in a festive mood. The horses with the carriages, the ammunition units and the gun carriage have all been assembled here. The men of the O-post are here too. The entire battery has come together.

The guns are still camouflaged and trained on the last target, but they are not loaded. The barrels are now being cleaned and thoroughly oiled. During the last days they served well and deserve care and peace.

This applies also to the horses, which enjoy the quietness at the shadowy rim of the woods. In addition to the fresh juicy grass of the meadows, the drivers have also provided a double ration of oats. The dusty and itching coat will finally be thoroughly cleaned with brush and curry-comb. Attentively the drivers wipe the horses' eyes and nostrils, and comb their manes and tails.

There is also opportunity for the bodily restoration of the men. The ponds in the meadow offering a refreshing bath. Next to it, in the shade of the alder, it is comfortable to rest. Tents have been set up. The sergeant and his men in charge of provisions have organized all sorts of delicacies either captured or purchased in the nearby village. There is an abundance of chocolate, cookies, an assortment of canned fish and meats, excellent delicatessen liverwurst, complemented by real and pure coffee—for the first time since the beginning of the war. Those who like it so may even drink it with sugar and milk. Gunner Buschhaus, our upright Saxon, happily smiles as he dips a piece of cake into the aromatic smelling contents of his field cup. In the evening every body gets in addition to the normal ration a boiled egg and an extra piece of butter. This lifts really the spirits.

What secret preparations are the gunners making there on the meadow? They are hauling logs, they are hauling brush wood. There is already a high pile. Nearby are a number of little barrels: two, three, four, five small barrels exactly lined up on blocks.

Today is midsummer night, a day of celebration of the summery time of nature and the holy fire in the night!

The preparations are interrupted one more time. One of the low armored caterpillar track vehicles of the French re-supply units is charging down the hill with a roaring motor and shattering caterpillar chains. Swerving in all direction between the tents around the woodpile. The men jump to all sides to escape the raving machine. Finally it stops down at the pond. From it the joker from Eastern Prussia, our Sergeant Katins, emerges all smiles about his successful prank.

The camp soon settles down again. It is a peaceful evening. The first stars shine on the eastern sky, whereas the west is still ablaze with the reds and violets of the sinking sun.

And then the flames of the midsummer night fire flare powerfully up from the dry brush and the resinous wood. In a circle around it the men of the battery have gathered—gunners and drivers, non-commissioned officers and officers. The song of the True Comrade echoes into the night. In deep thoughts the men stare into the flames.

Before any additional soldier and trooper songs, or fighting, happy and sad tunes could continue, the quiet voice of the battery chief comes out of the dark: "Comrades, we participated in something wonderful and great! What the German armies have achieved is so enormous that at first sight it appears to be a miracle. A country, which was considered the strongest military might in Europe, a country that in WWI could not be broken by the German blood and weapons in four years, this country has been completely defeated in a few weeks. However, we should remain modest and honest with ourselves: as enormous as the total accomplishment may be, in reality our individual achievements and sacrifices during our campaign are small and insignificant. We shall not forget that during the Great War of 1914 to 1918 in only one of the many fierce battles of materials, each individual had to accomplish much, much more than we all have today. They needed great bodily strength and endurance. Show firm resolution in the face of death, toughness and strength of character. Their acceptance of self denial is without comparison and they held high the faith in Germany and victory, in the face of all disappointments. We shall acknowledge thankfully and with admiration, that during the world war our fathers have set an example not yet reached by us. And we shall thank our superior and ingenious army leadership and the favorable fate, for enabling us, this time, to achieve such greatness without much sacrifice. We shall pledge that when we are called upon—sooner or later—we are ready for the greatest sacrifice, strongest loyalty, and greatest achievement!"

The End

EPILOGUE

The following is an excerpt from Wolf von Bleichert's final dictation (As recorded by his wife, Sighilt Seyler-von Bleichert, March 29, 1991), as related to his military service:

. . . I went to Czechoslovakia for a refresher course as artillery sergeant major. Together with my recruits I spent wonderful days in Prague. In June we rented the house of a head master of a school in Dresden. It was located in Koserow and had a beautiful garden where we harvested lots of asparagus and berries with the help of the three older boys. We were getting quite good at gardening. We often went dancing on the beach and in the restaurant by the beach, sometimes even on the pontoons in the water.

Then the war broke out. I refused to apply for exemption from military service as suggested by the company and reported to the 170th infantry regiment, which was assembling in Juteborg. We were initially stationed in the Saar region opposite the Maginot Line. Together with another sergeant major I was quartered in the house of a very nice lady.

In September 1939 we had rented a one-family house in Schoeneiche East of Berlin. We moved just in time from the house in Lichterfelde-Ost, because it got bombed shortly afterward. The house in Schoeneiche had a beautiful garden with fruit trees and a small pond where [my youngest son] Michael almost drowned one day. I remember that I used to take [my oldest son] Klaus to the children's service and afterward to an interesting museum. I also attended the Paradise Play together with him at the Christian Community. I still remember the huge farmer's hats the large cast supporting the choir was wearing.

In my military quarters I helped my hostess bake a big variety of Christmas cookies. She was very creative in this area.

Soon I was transferred within the battalion and assigned to the heavy battery. We had constructed a subterranean lookout on top of Schaltberg Mountain. We took turns standing guard and had a sweeping view of the entire French buffer zone. In between we went down to the neighboring village where I sometimes went on lookout from a window in a roof. There was not too much shooting going on at that time.

Not until spring when the snow cover gave way to tender green did we prepare to break through the Maginot Line. During the next six months I wrote a short book about this experience [the book you have just read].

After breaking through the Maginot Line we continued on to Nancy, Verdun and Lothringia. For me the campaign ended there. My division was transferred to Juteborg where we started systematic preparations for the war in the East. We stayed in a small village near Riepen where I conducted special training courses for non-commissioned officers. My squadron commander Captain Weirauch was a heavy drinker and I finally had to forsake all drinks and shots of any kind in order to save myself from too much alcohol. My hosts had a niece who accompanied me on wonderful rides on horseback to the heron nesting grounds. We also went swimming in the fishponds and took sleigh rides in winter. I was able to have my family visit from Berlin on a regular basis. Klaus was a real help during the potato harvest and [my second oldest son] Rolf pitched in as well. I used to meet my family at the train station in a horse-drawn carriage.

In the spring of 1941 we were transferred once again to the North of France near Amice to finish our training.

By now I had been promoted to the rank of lieutenant and was appointed as head of the gun squadron.

Together with the whole North-Eastern Prussian division we advanced to the Baltic States. We took some nice swims in the river Duena. In celebration of my daughter Maria's birth on July 12, 1941, I was able to treat my squadron to a whole wagonload of fresh strawberries sold to me by the local farmers.

Then came the first encounter with the enemy in a large wooded area where we suffered substantial losses. As an observer in the front line I was able to help carry our dead back to our lines. We moved ahead at a brisk pace from one firing position to the next. During one of these advances I ordered my troops to move ahead of me. While they were passing me the horse of a sergeant major kicked me in the lower shin. I marched on for a few more days when a squadron leader ordered me to the hospital where it was determined that I had broken the lower part of my shinbone. Before that I was attached to a commando and sent to a village where we had to arrest a number of suspects of some kind and transport them to a detention camp under supervision by a sergeant major. I was convinced that the suspects would undergo nothing more than extensive questioning once they got to the camp but that of course proved to be an illusion!

I was taken on a bumpy ride in a small truck, first to Reval and then on to Riega where I was put in the military hospital. I was in the same room with a severely wounded officer who was moaning night and day. After a few days I flew to Konigsberg in the copilot seat of a JU-50. We flew at very low altitude and the view was incredible. I was supposed to travel in a military hospital train via Berlin to the South Germany. I managed to stay behind at the Berlin train station and from there I took the subway to Schoeneiche where my family lived. The head of the military hospitals in Berlin was also our family doctor. I convinced him to take me on as an outpatient. I spent several months at home and used them to write my book on accident prevention, which was much in demand among employee advocates. It was soon out of print and the same publishing house published a second edition shortly after the end of the war.

After my release from the military hospital I was sent to a reserve regiment in Fuerstenwalde where they would have liked to keep me as an adjunct, which would have been quite feasible for a father of five children. But I wanted to get back to my old battalion, which had by then advanced to the Pogagnik valley on the outskirts of Leningrad.

I was appointed as head of the former 7th battery. We were stationed in the small village of Pogagnik, which was surrounded by a large wooded area. Each day I had to make a dash across an open field to get to my lookout point in the woods.

I was also able to scan the wooded area from the roof of the house where I was quartered. I stayed in contact with the company commander and the battalion. I had several bunkers in my field of vision.

One night a group of Russians worked its way through our lines and attacked our village from behind. Thanks to the fast reaction of a young sergeant our machineguns cut down all of the Russians. I was able to see some of the approaching Russians from my lookout point and my battery and I fought them successfully.

At noon we were attacked by a large number of tanks which came at us from the surrounding woods. I was able to detect them in time because of the movement of the trees. Our front line and my battery fought back and forth for hours. The tanks were unable to advance. They were, however, able to destroy our anti-tank guns, which were stationed in a barn in front of me. All through the following night we heard the Russians as they tried to rescue their damaged tanks. There were dead soldiers all along the periphery of the woods. They had been sitting on top of the tanks as they advanced. This afternoon brought me great recognition within the infantry.

We had our Russian prisoners dig a deep bunker on a hill outside the village. We reinforced it with thick man-size fir trees and equipped it with a water cistern and a stove. We lived there for quite a while in relative safety. Our lookout point was right outside the bunker.

There were dense fir trees on both sides of the road leading to the village. We were able to keep up contact with the rest of the battery because we could travel down that road without fear of being discovered. The entire cat population of the village congregated around the heated chimney at our house because the temperature outside was forty degrees below (Celsius). Every now and then we slaughtered some horses and feasted on the "cutlets." I also conducted training courses for my men. Thus we spent the winter of 1941/42 without any major incidents.

I was given the order to calibrate all of the big guns of the division. Together with my battery troops I moved from one lookout point to the next and was able to set up clean targets for the various batteries. Based on my calibration we were able to hit a number of Russian bunkers. Then it was decided to move one of the guns way out in front in order to be able to reach the area beyond the forest. To this end I and a troop of infantry men plus two radio operators made a foray deep into the woods where I found a tall iron pole that might have been used for land surveying purposes. From there I had a very good view and was able to reach some distant targets based on what I had observed. After that we beat a hasty retreat in order to avoid running into any Russian patrols. We managed very well.

A new phase of my service in the artillery started when I was assigned to lead my old 11th battery because the old battery commander had to be relieved. Soon afterward the whole division was moved. At first we had a period of rest which gave me the opportunity to successfully complete a whole battery maneuver under the watchful eye of the head of the division. Then we were deployed in Wolchow in a valley near St. Petersburg only to be moved once again and equipped with fresh horses, which came from Holland. We arrived in a little village amid a wooded area near Kolin and found ourselves right in partisan territory. Our veterinarian who had become my friend was shot and killed from behind while we were moving through the woods from battery to battery.

In a large wooded area we mounted a major attack on the Russians that was well prepared by our artillery. Unfortunately there were lots of land mines, which led to heavy losses on our side. Among others the sergeant major of our battery had his legs torn off. On the afternoon after the successful attack I was sitting in the underbrush with an infantry patrol when a so-called "Stalin Organ," consisting of a string of short-range grenades, struck in our immediate vicinity. Fortunately nobody was hit.

In the fall of 1942 it became apparent that as an engineer I should be deployed with a technical division rather than an equestrian one. Thus I was transferred to a railroad division even though, while being somewhat versed in cable cars I had no idea of bridge building, which was the main task of the railroad division. I was supposed to take over a cable car division in Vienna, which was used mainly for railroad and bridge construction. Thank God I had some highly skilled railway and bridge builders among my sergeants and non-commissioned officers. We drove for days clear across the south of Russia to Rostow on the Black Sea. We arrived just as the catastrophe of Stalingrad was happening and the German troops were streaming into Rostow . . .

Wolf von Bleichert died on May 9th 1991, prior to completion of this dictation.